The Behavioural Economics of Belarus

Praise for the Book

"Fiscal problems are a particular type of public choice in which not all stakeholders are included. Shifting global political, financial orders, globalization, all make this book a must-read not for just the current generation, but many more to come. It draws a lot of parallels between Belarus and China".

—Zhu Ning,

Professor of Finance, Tsinghua University, China; author of China's Guaranteed Bubble.

"To 'decode' traditionally has two meanings: to 'decipher', i.e., to find the meaning of something hidden behind symbols, and to 'deprogramme', i.e., to free from an imposed programme, from the spell of an inserted code. Kiryl Rudy's book copes brilliantly with the first aspect of decoding. It is to be hoped that the author will take an active part in the implementation of the second aspect of the process."

—Andrey Movchan

Director, Carnegie Moscow Center's Economic Policy Program, Russia.

"A bright look at the economy through the everyday values and stereotypes of modern Belarusians. It is original research which shows how cultural codes determine national economy and economic policy. It is a fascinating and easy read which will attract wide range of readers."

—Yulia Chernyavskaya

Author of *Belarusians: From 'tuteishyh' to Nation*, Belarus.

The Behavioural Economics of Belarus:

"Because We Decided So"

By

Kiryl Rudy

Cambridge Scholars
Publishing

The Behavioural Economics of Belarus: "Because We Decided So"

By Kiryl Rudy

This book first published 2020

Cambridge Scholars Publishing

Lady Stephenson Library, Newcastle upon Tyne, NE6 2PA, UK

British Library Cataloguing in Publication Data
A catalogue record for this book is available from the British Library

ISBN (10): 1-5275-5858-4
ISBN (13): 978-1-5275-5858-8

To my parents
In memory of my father

Contents

INTRODUCTION

In my student years, when I went to parties, discos, or Students' Day events, my father would often admonish me with sobering stories about fights ending in stab wounds, burnt corpses, and other frightening things. His stories stayed with me for a long time, rather than changing my mood just for the night. On the one hand, I have thought about that, and see that I believed my father, as a doctor and head of the emergency room, who was aware of admission department statistics. On the other hand, now I realise that there was something else behind his stories. These were his own childhood fears — during World War II he miraculously escaped fascists by hiding among typhoid patients, while some of our other relatives were shot for cooperating with partisans, and were not allowed to be buried, with their bodies left in the street for days. And his post-war relocation from Belarus to the east of the Urals in Russia, following my purged grandfather because the last was held captive by fascists during the war. And his choice of medical career, despite his haemophobia, as my grandfather was convinced that "only doctors survive when taken captive". This entanglement of the conscious and the unconscious made my father's stories vivid and crisp and affected my seemingly personal decisions and behaviour.

It is also sometimes unclear how the Belarusian economy behaves, how Belarusians make their economic decisions, and what affects such decisions — economic laws, personal experience, habits, phobias, intuition, mood, or something else. Or maybe all of these at a time? All the things that are daily 'encoded' in us in the form of information, emotions, or events, are then reproduced in our collective memory, grasp of the present, and vision of the future. In this way, our cultural environment forms the code that determines our economic behaviour. This is our economic code, our DNA, which is passed, not genetically, but socially. Therefore, a man's psyche and economic behaviour are determined by uploaded information, rather than by his nationality, race, or faith, i.e., something inherited.

Belarus, as well as its cultural matrix, is transformational, complex, and changeable. It is neither the Russian nor the European world. It tends to lean to the former and then to the latter. It fasts and then feasts.

It pulls back and then pushes ahead. It inspires hope and then brings depression. According to all reasonable economic laws, the economy of Belarus should have halted long ago, but its 'character' simultaneously saves and kills it. When one tries to understand it, and asks why this, or that, decision is taken, Belarusians respond with an indisputable argument — "because I decided so". The 'I' of every Belarusian combines into 'we', and then manifested in "Because we decided so". One can attempt to find, or come up with, a sound justification for this decision. But there is none. Just "I want, and I will", "I want to do it, not the best way, but my way". This puzzles further, and creates uncertainty.

It is obvious, however, that the behaviour of the Belarusian economy has its own logic, a clear desire to keep (even by force) the inherited post-Soviet structure and system of management. This gives a mental support point, and instils self-confidence and permissiveness. Such economic psyche is both individual and collective. The Belarusian society is characterised by a 'common sense syndrome' (also known as the 'Stockholm syndrome'), which describes joint engagement in behavioural economics. The Belarusian society is like a bird released from its cage — it does not fly away, fighting its desire to return. It is mesmerised by its memories, its familiar karma of suffering, and disappointment at the idealised freedom.

It is always a challenge to give a diagnosis to society. The problem is that people largely do not want to acknowledge it. It is not always pleasant to see oneself through others' eyes, to realise that one's psyche and behaviour are barriers rather than incentives for the economy. It's always easier to claim that, in the context of 'because we decided so', someone else, not 'we', decides everything for us and is to be blamed and bear the responsibility for everything. But this is not true. It's impossible to escape from oneself. One would not be able to hide behind the screen of the cultural matrix, public stereotypes, customary behaviour, '*pamiarkoŭnasć*' (forbearance – slow decision-making), '*možа tak i treba*' (maybe it is to be so – inherited humbleness), '*geta ŭsio roŭna ne maio*' (anyway, it's not my business – shifting responsibility), '*agulnaja mliavasć*' (fatigue), '*abyjakavasć da žyćcia*' (apathy), and other things. Such avoidance of decision-making is also a decision! Hence, "because I decided so", which forms "because we decided so", is the personal choice of every Belarusian. And this choice has certain consequences; it is necessary to bear responsibility for that choice, and it affects everyone; the entire Belarusian economy.

On the one hand, there is rational behavior based on financial abilities. On the other, 'normal' refers to a set of norms, habits, and traditions that has built up over time. Certainly, those two sides do not always see eye to eye, which is why it is important for each person to understand whether they are rational or normal.

Rational people always think and act correctly. They experience reasonable emotions. They evaluate risks as well as their own desires and abilities. They follow economic laws, responding appropriately to changes in prices, exchange rates, and interest rates. They plan out their lives, and those of their children, decades in advance. They value education as a profitable investment in human capital. They live strictly within their means. They are disciplined, they pay taxes, and they do not break the law. They stick to a diet (not only a financial one), eating food that, while healthy, does not always taste as good as they might like. They go for regular check-ups and do not try to treat themselves at home. They neither smoke nor drink alcohol. They are rational, if not always normal, people.

Normal people, for example, in Belarus, takes out large loans to buy the latest gadgets, electronic appliances, and expensive cars, pay for grand wedding celebrations and anniversaries, finance their trips abroad, and remodel their apartments. It is normal to borrow money to pay off loans and interest; they also borrow to finance their daily lives. It is normal to expect payment for doing nothing more than just showing up at work. It is normal to work and receive a pension at the same time. It is normal to value intellectual work less than physical labor. It is normal to make quick money. It is normal to risk public capital competing with private corporations. It is normal to confuse economic optimism with patriotism, work according to one's own rules, and live for today.

There is a unique understanding of fairness and an urge to be just like everyone else in Belarus: "they're no better than we are", "we have to save face", "don't be greedy and arrogant". This understanding, urge, and focus on getting fast results, as paradoxical as it may be, was born during a long period of stability. That led to a build-up of unused emotional and intellectual energy, as well as a confidence that many problems will take care of themselves at some point in an unknown future. In that context, all one can do is enjoy today and live for one's own satisfaction. A troubled past casts doubt on the future. Conservatism is born out of a desire to avoid mistakes, and new initiatives have to bear fruit immediately. Drawn-out economic problems lead to a pervasive depression, and expectations look no further than the short term.

There is no financial normalcy that holds true the world over. For example, in the US, borrowing to pay for university is normal. In China, whole families save up for old age, healthcare costs, or, for example, sending what is often their only child to study in the US. In Belarus, financial normalcy has changed with each of the last three generations.

The first is the Soviet generation. They consume little, appreciating above all what used to be hard to find. Those that lived through post-war hunger value food products. Others focus on household goods, the latest in fashion, and quality of life. Still others are more concerned with job stability than they are with their salary. When it comes to economic problems, they blame everyone but themselves.

The second is the post-Soviet generation raised by their Soviet parents. They lived through perestroika, the wild 1990s, and the rich 2000s. They value the wider opportunities that come with meeting new, more expensive demands: cars, homes, and tourism. They make up a consumer-based society in which individual values crowd out public values. Consumerism is the currency of success. Their behavior is based on individual survival ("Who cares, so long as it doesn't affect me?") with minimal socialization, annoyance at those around them, a trust deficit, and suspicion toward success, and each other.

The third is the modern generation born in independent Belarus. They make up the middle class as well as civil society. Yes, they carry on the individual values of their parents as well as their overinflated social expectations. On the other hand, they are taking more and more responsibility for cultivating themselves and getting the older generations accustomed to social values: national culture, language, sovereignty, healthcare, education, sports, the environment, public order. There is an internal struggle between individual and social values, one in which the winner is tough to predict.

The three generations all have in common a desire to move from state capitalism to a human capitalism that prioritizes individual and social values. At the heart of that system is human capital, civil society, and the welfare state. Only a glimpse of the future, hope, trust, well-founded optimism, and the everyday banality of common sense and kindness will foster growth and prosperity.

The Belarusian economy has been stagnating since 2015, though, paradoxically, stagnating systems can maintain stability for quite a while. In Belarus' case it boils down to the values and habits of each generation: those who lived through the tough times would probably not mind suffering a little to avoid the war, hunger, deficit, and other memories haunting them from the Soviet and post-Soviet years. The second generation would be more reticent to slip back into recession, having once tasted shopping tours and sunny holidays at the beach. A lack of experience makes the reaction of the third generation hard to predict, as it happened after the President's election in August 2020, when this generation raised the whole country to become politically active.

This book concerns the approach to decoding the economy, changing the determinism of the psyche and behaviour. The common perception is that it would take centuries, decades at best, as new values are to come with the arrival of new generations. But new values will not appear by themselves. Things embedded are then reproduced. And nowadays it is quite a quick process. The time needed to apprehend new information is rapidly diminishing. It used to take years, now it takes a few months. For instance, when a person gets to a foreign country, with a different cultural matrix, he intuitively feels the difference, and adapts quickly, owing to his instinct for self-preservation. Similarly, when the country's economic climate changes, people will inevitably adapt. The only thing that matters is that the goal of transformation should be their improved wellbeing, rather than some other non-economic goals.

In a nutshell, decoding leads to transparency and openness. To achieve that, the economy needs to 'turn on the light' and 'open the door', creating an understandable and favourable climate for foreign investors, in the first place. They serve as a channel for the transfer to Belarus not only of money, technology, and expertise, but also – most importantly – of universal international values, which transform national models of behaviour, highlight advantages, and form the features necessary for the transformation of behavioural economics into classical economics.

This book is the non-economic answer to the economic challenges faced by Belarus in recent decades. Let me briefly explain the logic behind my working as Economic Advisor in President's Administration in 2013 – 2016 and why classical economic instruments (I called them "The Financial Diet") didn't work for economic reforms in Belarus.

First, I used to think that budget constraints would create sound incentives in the Belarusian economy. If the monetary conditions were tightened (through balancing the budget, bringing inflation down, quenching devaluation expectations), then the remaining budget funds would flow, not to state-owned enterprises, but to the state – to finance the social sphere, security, and public administration. I assumed that if there was no wind, one would have to row. In other words, a deficit of financial resources would push economic reforms and preserve social stability. I expected that, to avoid a recession caused by a lack of budget financing, the economy would open up for private and foreign investments. But that did not happen. The economy was in recession, while there were no reforms and subsequent investments. Decision-making was led not by economic incentives, but by something else – habits, instincts, and stereotypes. The forceful conservatism and the desire to stop and wait surfaced in the context of stronger economic uncertainty and difficulties with understanding it. But that results only in retarding the future and lagging further behind.

Second, I expected that the technocratic approach was working. Figuratively speaking, if one fixed a single grain of sand, one would be able to prevent an avalanche. If we adopted certain decisions on specific projects, without changing the 'abstract' business climate, we would be able to avoid a crisis. And then, the mix of separate decisions would generate a tangible effect for the whole economy. But this gives only a sense of effect. It's like walking around in a dark room with a candle. It is impossible to capture everything and create favourable conditions for everyone in this way. But the issue is not that the Belarusian economy does not work in such conditions. It does! Unsustainably and slowly. It adapts in any case, acquiring hybrid features. The issue is rather whether the economy is the main goal for Belarus. There are different economic models, including those with low living standards, vague prospects, which are, however, acceptable for the public. Hence, the society focuses not on economic, but on other priorities, which become a barrier to the economy. And if it is true, everyone – not a single, but every grain of sand – is to blame when an avalanche strikes.

Third, time seemed to be the main factor of change. If the internal conditions for economic reforms are ripe, the external factors are pushing towards that, and there is a team of like-minded people, it is the best time. However, this is not enough. Social aspirations and political will are uppermost. It is precisely the combination of social and political activity oriented in the same direction that could generate coordinated 'pulsing', pushing economic growth. Or that could be held back, accumulating until breakthrough is possible. Or could spread evenly, ensuring economic stability. In addition to social and political activity, another essential element is economists. Even under some ideal conditions, decisions are made by people often under the influence of socio-cultural, rather than economic, factors. It reduces the demand for economists, leading to their outflow to other areas and a drop in the overall level of competence in the economy. As a result, more and more problems surface in the economy, like in a shoaling pond. Therefore, it is not time, but activity and competence that are vital to reform the Belarusian economy, establishing an upward trend in its growth.

All these misconceptions have shaped the need to take a broader approach, and look at the Belarusian economy not only from the point of view of an economist. International readers also have an opportunity to look at Belarusians and their economic behaviour from a different angle. Would they recognise them, accept the assessments and proposals? When I stand in their shoes, re-reading the introduction, I get to see a vague image of something strange and familiar in the text. There are my running medical metaphors (diet, diagnosis), probably popping up from the depths of my childhood memories under the influence of my father and other relatives, who worked in the medical field. And the term the 'Stockholm syndrome', which is used here for some reason, and resonates only too well with my grandfather's "only doctors survive when taken captive". Even now, it is difficult to find a simple and reasonable explanation why those expressions and comparisons have come up in particular, and why I have undertaken to write this book. The first answer that comes, and stays deep inside, is "because I decided so". Such answers form something bigger, the cultural matrix of Belarus – "because we decided so".

CHAPTER 1

THE CULTURAL MATRIX

Introduction

In April 2016, as Economic Advisor to the President of the Republic of Belarus together with other Belarusian regulators, I had a few meetings with foreign investors and holders of Belarusian government bonds within the framework of the Spring Meetings of the International Monetary Fund and the World Bank, in Washington. In one of the meetings, foreign investors asked me very straightforward questions: "Will there be economic reforms in Belarus or not?" "What do you think about it?" "We hear contradictory statements. How should we understand you, Belarusians?" The investors got seemingly satisfactory responses from me as a member of the Belarusian delegation: "It is more important what we do, rather than what we think or say! If we implement tax, pension, and other reforms, you see that. Therefore, the main thing is how we behave, the main thing is our behaviour."

In June 2018, as Ambassador of Belarus in China, I gave a lecture to Chinese generals and admirals at the Chinese Academy of National Defence. After my diplomatic speech about Belarus and Sino-Belarus relations, one of the high-level Chinese officers asked a very interesting question: "How come, that during economic recession and the fall of incomes in your country, Belarusians don't go out to protest and strike in the streets?" My answer was the following: "There is one behavioural trick. When you jump in the hot tub, you immediately jump out. But if you get in the hot water slowly you'll get used to that and stay there".

These two stories can briefly characterise the Belarusian cultural matrix and its impact on the economy — the behaviour of Belarusians forms the behavioural economics of Belarus.

Behavioural economics is not unique to Belarus.[1] Back in 1953, Milton Friedman, a Nobel Memorial Prize laureate in Economic Sciences, used an apt analogy in this context — when a snooker player makes a shot, he hardly considers the laws of geometry and physics, and similarly, when making economic decisions, he is unlikely to be guided by statistics and economic laws in his behaviour.[2] In classical economics, it is assumed that one would act logically and reasonably in extreme cases – intuitively relying on knowledge, statistics and experience. Sometimes one makes mistakes, of course, under the influence of emotions, but it rarely happens, since it is believed that one controls oneself so these errors can be neglected.

In theory, everything is supported with facts and statistics, and established patterns should become norms and stereotypes of human behaviour, i.e. the theory of classical (non-emotional) economics. But, in practice, the opposite is often true. All our emotions, speculations, norms, and stereotypes, take possession of us, and lead us, interpreting reality, new facts, statistics, and consistent patterns. We make everything that happens around us fit our mood, and our conception of the surrounding world; we interpret facts through the prism of our beliefs; we build everything into our cultural matrix, distorting new phenomena and facts. Thus, in behavioural economics, it is often the theory that shapes the practice of our behaviour, rather than the practice that shapes the theory. As a result, everything is reversed in behavioural economics. 'Theoreticians' are those who cannot cope with their beliefs, habits, or memories, and are trapped in their 'theories'. While 'practitioners' are those who change and adapt to the new reality, relying on continuously arriving new knowledge, facts, and statistics.

So, behavioural economics is economics based on real-world practice, with its irrationality, emotions, social norms and stereotypes of people's behaviour. Unlike classical economics, which relies on smart incentives, logical (easy) choice, laws of minimising risks and maximising benefits (values), behavioural economics is empirical economics based on facts, experiments, established practices, prejudices and decisions, sometimes made in an unreasonable, intuitive and chaotic way, in the environment of market and government failures. The similarity between behavioural and classical economics is that the irrationality of the former is also regular, repeatable, and predictable, in its own way, which enables its study and application of scientific methods.

Studies of behavioural economics through the prism of interrelations between culture and economics trace their lineage to the classical works of Adam Smith, John Stuart Mill, Karl Marx, and Max Weber,[3] and are further undertaken today by modern Israeli, American, and European scientific schools.[45] Given that it is mathematically difficult to give a straightforward description of interrelationships between culture and economics, mathematical economists tend not to be very interested in this field, yielding it to economic sociologists and economic psychologists. In this regard, the science of behavioural economics has become best known in identifying interrelationships based on examples of certain economic activities and target groups of people, for instance in the field of finance.[67] In particular, the fundamental and technical analysis of financial markets is nothing more than a study of respectively classical and behavioural economics of finance. Attempts to apply behavioural economics at the national level, and estimate the influence of the cultural matrix on the entire economy, disclose the need to take a broader view, with cross-disciplinary research carried out in the fields of sociology, cultural studies, history, psychology, and other areas.

Economics is only part of our life. Behavioural economics, the economic code, is also only one element, a branch of something bigger, more general – the cultural matrix.

The cultural matrix — defined as the habitus by French sociologist Pierre Bourdieu — is understood here as the collective programming of psyche and behaviour.[89] Ordinary people may sometimes call it the 'national character'. This system includes values, habits, norms, rules, behavioural practices, and stereotypes, cultural implications that are common to a group of people. The cultural matrix depends on the human environment — the society, politics, economics, laws, institutions, and nature, i.e. everything that surrounds a person. Therefore, people representing different cultures have different perceptions of what is normal, valuable and functioning. Something that is considered common sense and acceptable in one culture seems strange, and is rejected, in another. Differences in thinking are reflected in differences in languages, actions, behaviour, appearance, and even facial expressions. The variety of cultural matrices always enables comparisons to be made, and conclusions to be drawn about the distinctive features of this or that matrix.

The concept of the cultural code also appears in this book. It is seen here as a form of transmission of the cultural matrix and its elements in the process of communication, when the cultural code is used to decode elements of the cultural matrix, for instance cultural implications, stereotypes and behavioural practices. When the cultural matrix interacts with economics and economic relations, the economic code, which characterises our economic psyche and behaviour, is displayed.

The Cultural Matrix in Various Fields of Science

The cultural matrix is quite a complex system that is studied in different ways by different sciences, ranging from medicine to mathematics.

In the field of neuroscience, the cultural matrix is usually studied in the limbic system of the brain. According to Paul MacLean's theory of the 'Triune Brain', the human brain can be divided into three complexes: limbic, reptilian, and cognitive. The limbic complex is responsible for emotions, memory, instincts, charm, sleep, wakefulness, and the functioning of internal organs. This is the complex that characterises the socialisation of humans. The reptilian complex regulates the basic vital activities: breathing, pulse, body temperature and some primitive emotions, such as fear and aggression. The cognitive complex, that accounts for 80% of the brain, is responsible for abstraction, the ability to think and speak, and to analyse and make rational decisions. The attribution of the cultural matrix to the limbic complex is explained by mental convenience; the comfort of passivity. Although the cognitive complex occupies most of the brain, the limbic complex of the human brain appeared earlier, has developed longer, and is estimated to influence decision-making by 95%.[10] It should be noted that, although the theory of the 'Triune Brain' is useful, it is not universal. Other research methods are also used, for instance monitoring the human pupil's response to his thinking and behaviour, as driven by the cultural matrix.[11] The human brain has yet to be properly studied and is complex to understand. In this context, behavioural reflexes are sometimes studied through the reaction of animals most similar to humans, as well as the evolution of living beings. In general, studies of the cultural matrix are essential for neuroscience, as well as for cross-disciplinary areas at the interface of psychology, sociology, culture studies, political science, and economics.

In the field of psychology, the cultural matrix is studied as an element of human unconscious behaviour. Proposed theories are tested on representative groups, being proved or disproved. In the theory of behaviourism, humans are viewed as information systems.[12] They accumulate information using all their senses and then reproduce it. When the available information is utilised to build logical chains, their actions are rational. But when there is more information than can be comprehended, the unconscious cultural matrix is triggered. Under its influence, humans try to adjust the reality to their beliefs, habits, norms, and stereotypes, and act automatically, unconsciously selecting similar scenarios from their memory and reproducing them to obtain the expected result. At the same time, they hardly realise they are behaving irrationally, 'going around in circles'. Everything seems familiar and logical in its own way. Paradoxically, this is combined with our desire to manage and control everything. In view of this, it is sometimes scary that the unconscious can guide us. So, in fact, we do not always manage and control ourselves and our decisions. Since the human brain is unable to embrace all the necessary facts, probabilities, and figures, in the process of decision-making, people think in words, sentences, and stories, which indicates the predominance of the emotional over the rational in us. In this case, big decisions are often chaotic, formed under the influence of random external events and the things and people we hear, see, or encounter at that moment. Small decisions, in their turn, characterise the internal logic of psyche and behaviour. In psychology, it is the chain of small decisions that characterises the cultural matrix.

In the fields of sociology and social psychology, the cultural matrix is viewed in terms of the way individuals' mentalities interact, and social orientations are formed. The latter create a 'lens' through which society sees reality and reacts to it. There is a range of social orientations: collectivism or individualism, paternalism or liberalism, masculinity or feminism, chaos or uncertainty avoidance, short-term or long-term planning, high or low level general credibility, the attitude toward risk, self-expression and survival,[13] the process or the result, universality or specialisation, emotional expressiveness or emotional restraint,[14] multi-activity, reactivity or linear activity,[15] and past, present, or future.[16] For example, orientation to the past makes one recall old practices to solve current problems. Nostalgia leads to repetition and imitation. Orientation to the present results in emotionality, impulsiveness, impatience for results, and evasion of long-term decisions. Orientation to the future results in regularity, order, and greater rationality. In other words, under the impact of its orientations, the society follows the general flow of stereotypes and platitudes that shape its current cultural status.

In the fields of cultural studies, ethnology and anthropology, the cultural matrix is studied in the framework of ethnicity and identity. At the same time, there can be collective, individual, and group ethnicity. The cultural matrix can be classified as collective unconscious ethnicity, which is also called mentality. It is formed under the influence of everyday life, and unconsciously teaches a person 'what is good' and 'what is bad'.[17] Ethnologists place special emphasis on the unconsciousness of the cultural matrix, which helps the population maintain the integrity and specific orientation of their psyche and behaviour. The ethnic culture includes two types of values – the propensity for development (change) and the propensity for stability (affirmation), which alternate under the impact of external challenges. There are also studies that connect human values and behaviour with religion, and outline the limits of tolerance and the nature of religious fanaticism.[18]

In the field of political science, the cultural matrix is most often found in studies on informal institutions, nationalism, and authoritarianism. In the context of underdeveloped institutions, where the credibility of the government and society is low, family, friends, informal and traditional ties, and social capital, gain greater value. In such conditions, the cultural matrix becomes the driver of behaviour. It serves as the basis for manifesting nationalism, populism, and authoritarianism, which are opposed to multiculturalism, rationalism, and democracy. However, such opposition tends to be temporary, as all political systems somehow move towards democracy and pluralism, but at a different pace. The more deeply rooted the cultural matrix is, the more difficult it is to embrace other cultures, and the slower the movement of society towards democracy. Moreover, in the environment of populism and authoritarianism, the cultural matrix becomes more deeply rooted. Popular politicians themselves try to approach it, and relay it back to the public, who respond by adjusting. As a result, the cultural matrix becomes closed and less decodable. Amid the fear of cultural shock and mental discomfort, the cultural matrix strengthens, and can turn into a barrier to society's ability to adapt to change and even to survive. In this regard, the role of politicians is to be able to help people perceive reality, inspire hope, and mobilise for adaptation, in other words – to change the cultural matrix, saving it from itself.

In economics, the cultural matrix is studied within the framework of the economic cycle.[19] "In the economic boom phase, the cultural matrix is loaded with resources, can afford cultural and social experiments, for instance democratisation, personal autonomy, and gender equality. At the peak of economic growth, a certain social balance prevails over rational thinking that does not support further economic growth and creates conditions for conservative stagnation. In the environment of an economic recession, the cultural matrix can yield to rational behaviour based on the sense of self-preservation of the society. At the same time, political will is essential to suppress the cultural matrix in order to recover economic growth. However, as political will is manifested under the influence of political and socio-cultural, rather than economic factors, it may be trapped within the cultural matrix. The closer politicians are to the cultural matrix the more popular they are, the greater support they get from the population, and the more difficult it is to get out of the matrix to lift the cultural barriers to economic growth. This is mainly the reason why popular leaders (populists, demagogues, nationalists) often remain in the collective memory for a long time, although they tend to bring their countries to economic disaster (Joseph Stalin, Mao Zedong, Nicolae Ceauşescu, Slobodan Milošević, Hugo Chavez, to name a few).

In the field of information technology, the cultural matrix becomes a new environment in the social networks, like Facebook and Twitter, to get big behavioural data, to machine learn them, and predict the behaviour of users. In the book *Age of Surveillance Capitalism*, by Harvard professor Shoshana Zuboff, it's mentioned that IT platforms like Facebook, Instagram, and others, use automated machine processes to not only know our behaviour, but also shape our behaviour at scale.[20] With this reorientation from knowledge to power, it's no longer enough to automate information flows about people; the goal now is to automate them, and instead of labor, surveillance capitalism uses every aspect of every human's experience.

In the field of mathematics, the socio-cultural mentality and behaviour of the population (among other things in economics) are studied in the light of the theory of 'games of strategy', developed by John von Neumann.[21] The application of the mathematical apparatus to socio-cultural and economic processes has natural limitations related to knowledge, imperfections in the description of facts, uncertainty of terminology, vagueness of formulated problems, and absence of quantitative measures. Therefore, the cultural matrix is studied, element by element, in mathematics, with simple interdependencies of behaviour built, and with progressive movement towards more complex interrelationships. As the mathematical apparatus develops further, the interest of mathematical economists shifts from the cultural matrix to other problems, which they see as more urgent. At present, despite the availability of modern computer mathematical simulation software, mathematics is still inferior to other scientific methods, such as a thorough description of facts, in the field of comprehensive investigation of the entire cultural matrix. In this regard, the most typical and effective tools for studying the cultural matrix are verbally expressed humanitarian statements, rather than precise mathematical evidence.

The Cultural Matrix: Features

Given the diversity of scientific theories, it should be noted that the cultural matrix is complex, and has many dimensions to study. A common cross-disciplinary denominator for its investigation can be found in the Complex Systems Theory, the Theory of Chaos, Bayes' Theorem (its formula was accidentally found in Thomas Bayes' records after he died in 1761), Bernoulli's Equation, the law of 'large numbers', 'The Butterfly Effect' formulated by Edward Lorenz, the methods of assessing the collective memory, historical analogies, scientific descriptions, and so on.

The cultural matrix is a complex dynamic system, which most often depends on past events. Thus, when studying it, it is first necessary to take into account the information previously known within the framework of this culture, and then weigh and structure it, factoring in the values of the society.

The study of the cultural matrix is simplified by the fact that its agents are, on average, similar, share common values, prefer interaction within their group, tend to make decisions, and shape their behaviour based on known past events. In addition, the information filling the matrix is limited to the existing generations and the values circulating between them. Within the cultural matrix, there is undoubtedly some diversification of social values, depending on sex, age, education, income, occupation, place of residence, and so on. However, cultural factors still prevail in the formation of common values and are easier to explore.

The fact that the cultural matrix is an open system complicates its scientific understanding, making it incomplete and deceptive. Therefore, it is also necessary to assess the probability of events, which could occur in their own right, based on incoming new information, and the interaction of this cultural matrix with others. In view of its openness, the cultural matrix is constantly engaged in the process of self-reflection and adaptation, thus it is unpredictable. It may change the structure of its agents, the weights of values in the system, or accept new elements with unknown influence on the whole system. In this regard, the cultural matrix is unstable and unbalanced, and can, surprisingly quickly, plunge into chaos all the way down to self-destruction. At the same time, the risk of disintegration of the cultural matrix depends on its size and the speed at which its representatives adjust to changes. In view of this, specific qualities, such as flexibility and dynamism, are to be studied separately.

The cultural matrix is a very flexible system that changes both vertically and horizontally, going beyond national boundaries.

Vertically, it manifests itself in the process of education and the transfer of cultural values to children within their family. The cultural matrix becomes most deeply rooted in a person during childhood, when he is most influenced by it. Family-orientation nurtures collectivism, opposing 'us to them'. The division of people into 'friends' and 'foes', who are correspondingly seen as 'good' and 'bad', begins within the family. In addition, the negative attitude towards 'foes' is more pronounced than the positive attitude toward 'friends', and the understanding that both leagues include both 'bad' and 'good' ones is dulled. This lays the foundations of social discrimination, which is then unconsciously reproduced in relation to people representing a different cultural matrix, country, nation, race, faith, body build, and sexual and other orientations. This dulls traits such as openness and tolerance.

Horizontally, the cultural matrix extends along with the expansion of the circle of trust. It goes beyond the family circle, covering educational institutions, professional, religious, and other elements of one's social environment. In this regard, members of respective groups develop cultural and mental similarity and increased trust, for instance, between graduates of one form, school, group, university, and between different people of the same profession or religion. This is the way the structure of the cultural matrix is formed with the values, behavioural practices, and other elements of different groups.

Horizontally, the cultural matrix can cross borders, spreading to several countries, becoming regional and global.

The regional cultural matrix is formed by entangled national values, typically those of neighbouring countries.[22] Depending on the country, elements of a certain national matrix may dominate in the regional matrix. Examples of regional cultural matrices include: the European (EU countries), American (US, Canada), Soviet (USSR), Russian (Russian-speaking countries), Asian (PRC, Southeast Asian countries), and African (Central and Southern Africa) matrices. The regional matrix can suppress national ones, for example, the Soviet matrix. After the collapse of the Soviet Union, it seemed that there would be regional decoding and that the national matrices would revive. Twenty five years on, it is obvious that in a few post-Soviet countries the regional matrix has not disappeared, it has been transformed.

The global cultural matrix is formed under the influence of universal values, fashion, openness, mobility of information, people, goods, technologies, and the interpenetration of national and regional matrices.[23] Different ideas have unsuccessfully aspired to the status of the global matrix. In the early and mid-20th century, those were conservatism, communism, and fascism. In the 1980s and 1990s, it was liberalism, in the 2000s, pragmatism, and in the 2010s, populism. These ideas extended to different countries, fired the imagination, became popular, spanning entire continents. National matrices have also attempted to play the role of the global one. The globalisation of the 1990s and 2000s, for instance, was often perceived as Americanisation, accompanied by an expansion of American values. With the rise of the PRC's role in the world economy, the global importance of the US has become less obvious. Thus, the global matrix cannot be monocultural. It is always multicultural and preaches universal values: openness, transparency, tolerance, pluralism, etc. Venice and Genoa in the past, and Hong Kong and Singapore today, could be mentioned as real examples of global multicultural matrices.

The cultural matrix is a fairly dynamic system that can change at different rates, both in an evolutionary and a revolutionary way, depending on the adaptation of its individual agents to change.

When generations 'digest' historic events, political regimes, revolutions, wars, new technologies, urbanisation, transformations of the middle class, and the aging of the population, it is transmitted and developed in an evolutionary way. If we take the structure of society, businesses respond to change first. They operate in a competitive environment, where changes trigger smart incentives, and the instinct of self-preservation pushes them to adapt faster than everyone else. Then follows the civil society (non-governmental organisations), the family, and the government. Religious institutions are the slowest in responding to change.[24]

A revolutionary change (break) in the cultural matrix implies a transition to a different matrix. The techniques of the so-called 'colour revolutions' usually include such elements as the involvement of foreign non-governmental organisations in the preparation of coups d'état, ideological discrediting of government, consolidation of supporters through social networks, and choosing the moment of social instability to mobilise mass public support. However, it is important to consider not so much the techniques and triggers, but rather the causes and the driving force of the break in the cultural matrix. As a rule, the causes include social inequality and long-lasting economic depression. In turn, the main driver of revolutionary change is typically the younger (third) generation, which is most sensitive to change and is characterised by low fear barriers – the so-called 'unwhipped generation'. It is the demographic shift and the opening of the 'age window' of the active population which are used by many researchers to explain the 'colour revolutions' of recent years.[25][26]

In summary, the cultural matrix is a complex, open, flexible, and dynamic system of values that determines national features. The national matrix is formed under the influence of a variety of natural, geographical, historical, cultural, religious, racial, age, linguistic, political, economic, and other factors. It is noteworthy that, sometimes due to short-term and superficial reasons, certain features are fixed in the culture, determining the psyche and behaviour and sticking for a long time as a label (most often negative) used to describe the cultural matrix. For example, the opinions that Asians are hardworking, Africans are lazy, the Chinese are Asian Jews, and Jews, in their turn, are cunning, smart, successful businessmen, that Germans are disciplined, the French are stylish, the British are mannered and formal, Americans are unique, Latinos are cheerful, Russians are doomed to suffer, Ukrainians are impudent and cunning, Belarusians are greedy, and so on. The national specifics of behaviour are sometimes generalised, in quite a sketchy way, through the manners of driving – observance of traffic regulations; civility to others, such as those driving more expensive cars, cyclists, pedestrians; frequency of warning signals; speed; etc. To take a few examples, the observed chaotic traffic discipline in China and India is characterised by the 'common sense' of being the first, but avoiding conflicts; in the former Soviet Union countries, it is the inevitability of punishment, observance of the rules 'no matter what'; while in Western Europe it is mutual respect and a general understanding of fairness and traffic manners.

National features can be explained in different ways. For example, in the early 20th century, German sociologist Max Weber noted that the determinant of the social and economic successes of Germany and Switzerland was the fact that people in these countries were Protestants, unlike in the less successful Southern European countries inhabited by Catholics.[27] The success of Southeast Asian countries and China, in recent decades, is often explained by the Confucian values and diligence inherent in their people. The problems of a number of Arab and Muslim countries are sometimes explained by their overestimated self-esteem, national pride, and painful apprehension of others' superiority, which leads to the perception of reality through the lens of "who did this to us?" rather than "why am I what I am?".[28] Cultures are sometimes grouped depending on whether they gravitate towards, or resist, progress. For example, it is justified that Protestantism is much more conducive to modernisation than Catholicism, especially in the Western Hemisphere;

Confucianism is more conducive to development than Islam, Buddhism, or Hinduism; Orthodox Christianity is similar to Catholicism, but Orthodox countries still gravitate to communism, etc. In general, Jews, Confucians, and Protestants are considered the most progressive.[29] At the same time, some scientists argue that the higher the urbanisation, the lower the level of religious devotedness, and the more open and more highly-educated the country is, the more it relies on international norms and laws, and the less it depends on its cultural matrix.[30][31]

Is There a Cultural Matrix?

The theoretical controversy and complexity of the cultural matrix sometimes cause reasonable doubt as to whether it exists at all.[32][33] Could it be merely self-induced public hypnosis, some mythical explanation of complex socio-economic phenomena? For example, there are a few studies pointing at the fact that there is no correlation between the 'national character' and personality traits.[34] Another example is the research approach based on studying the behaviour of migrants from different countries within one country, which also calls into question the impact of the cultural matrix of the recipient country on migrants. In this case, the social circle plays a greater role in adaptation to the new matrix, rather than the whole new cultural matrix itself.[35] In the popular book *Outliers,* by Malcolm Gladwell, the secret of the success of certain individuals is also explained by the time they spent in education and on the development of their practical skills, rather than by their belonging to a particular nation.[36] In the provocative book *Blank Slate*, by Harvard professor Steven Pinker, he insists that the inherited values play the main role in human behaviour rather than collected values in cultural environment.[37]

Another example is the ideology of multiculturalism and internationalism based on the equality and interaction of nations as an alternative to the proletarian internationalism of Marxism, nationalism, and globalism. If there are generally accepted international universal human values, then they become the priority, prevailing over national ones, which calls into question the need for the national cultural matrix. If there are international threats to national matrices (terrorism, biological and social diseases, the proliferation of weapons of mass destruction, etc.), they bring the national matrices together within the framework of a common international platform, reducing the value of the former.

The cultural matrix includes a set of values, behavioural practices, stereotypes, and other elements and, thus, can be regarded in some sense as something generally irrational, unconscious, and unstable, that can be changed. *And if it is subject to influence and can be changed, then does it exist at all?*

In his hypothesis of 'path dependence', Russian economist Alexander Auzan relies on the research by Richard D. North to prove how a country and its economy could escape from the cultural rut, i.e. the cultural matrix.[38][39] The countries that are stuck in the cultural rut have three similarities:

1) the elites create laws for others, and exceptions for themselves;
2) for-profit, political, and non-profit organisations are built around individuals, and die with them; and
3) the tools of violence are distributed among groups of elites.

The countries whose economies have managed to overcome the barrier of the cultural rut, having proved the non-existence of the cultural matrix, in their turn they have the opposite similarities:

1) the elites create laws for themselves and expand them to cover others;
2) for-profit, political, and non-profit organisations outlast their creators;
3) the elites jointly exercise control over the tools of violence.

Examples of the latter countries and territories include Japan, Singapore, Taiwan, Hong Kong, and Korea.

In practice, the importance of the cultural matrix is sometimes distorted in the public perception, which at times justifies both national superiority and humiliation (even genocide), for example with the Romans, Mongols, Japanese, Chinese, 'Aryans', Armenians, and Jews. At the same time, the existence of the cultural matrix and its impact on the economy are questioned, based on convincing historical examples of people of one nation or one culture diverging in their economic development within different times, or even within the same period.

Sweden. Prior to the openness and reforms carried out by Minister of Finance Johan August Gripenstedt in the 1860s, it had been a poor country, not only by European standards, but even poorer than the

Congo. Only after decoding and opening up the country and its economy did Sweden enter the so-called era of '100 years of growth'.

Argentina. In 1870-1914, Argentina boasted the highest GDP growth in the world – about 6% per year – due to the openness of its economy, migration of labour resources from Italy, inflow of foreign investment, and the export of beef and wheat. In 1914, Argentina was one of the ten richest countries in the world, ahead of Germany and France. The situation changed after the country turned to the policies of protection of national values, import substitution, restrictions on the movement of capital, and reinforced state controls. This led to a century of Argentina falling behind.

Japan. In the *Japan Herald*, a Japanese newspaper, one can find the following quote, dated 1881: "Wealthy we do not at all think [Japan] will ever become: the advantages conferred by nature, … and the love of indolence and pleasure of the people themselves, forbid it. The Japanese are a happy race, and being content with little, are not likely to achieve much." It is noteworthy, that as early as the 16th century, the isolated Japanese society nearly reached a fatal extreme when it denounced firearms (considering guns an invention of strangers). But the opening of Japanese ports for foreign trade, and the introduction of advanced Western standards, put an end to the centuries-long isolation of the country and placed it among the world leaders. At present, there are renewed attempts in Japan to pursue the policy of "one race, one civilisation, one language, and one culture", which serves as a contradictory explanation of both the past achievements and the current slowdown in the country's development.

France. In the 1890s, import substitution, and the introduction of high tariffs for agricultural imports, led to higher food prices, increased wages in this sector, growing birth rates in rural areas, abandonment of education, and lower urbanisation. In the long run, it resulted in a declining middle class and poorer human development, with the economy of Britain, which pursued the opposite policy, outperforming France's during the early 20th century.[40]

Spain. The period of Franco's dictatorship (1939-1975) can be divided into two periods: the first one, lasting twenty years until 1959, and the second one following it, when economic reform began. For ten years, a stabilisation plan was implemented aimed at ensuring the openness and liberalisation of the economy. In the late 1960s, political reforms began: the law on the press was adopted, local self-government was expanded, and non-political strikes were allowed. According to a few researchers, it was the economic openness that started, and led to a transformation of, the culture of thinking and behaviour of Spaniards and eventually laid the foundation for the country's further social and economic success.[41]

Germany and Korea. One cannot help recalling the social experiments, in the framework of the same cultural environment, that were carried out within the same period of time, in former West and East Germany,[42] and which are still running in South Korea and the DPRK. These examples demonstrate the socio-economic differences between people of the same culture. In the case of Korea, it is also remarkable that relatively recently (in the 1960s), North Korea was better economically developed than South Korea. And speaking of Germany, of course, there are obvious contradictions in the one cultural matrix of Nazi and modern Germany, or, by analogy, in fascist and modern Italy. Interestingly, these examples inspire optimism about the prospects of decoding the Soviet man in Russia, Belarus, and other post-communist countries.

China and Russia. The cyclical nature of China's economic development over two centuries can be explained by politics, economics, openness, and isolation, but certainly not by its national features. At one point in time, the Chinese invented the compass, paper, and gunpowder, while at another point in time, they renounced ocean navigation, mechanical clocks, and spinning looms. Just like in China, with its rejection and return to religion, closeness, and openness, Russia's culture did not play a decisive role in the country's development, be it before, during, or after the USSR. At the same time, judging by the differences in the dynamics, size, and structure of their economies over the past thirty years, China and Russia have proved that the key factors of a country's development are its openness and adaptability, rather than its ideology and culture.

Thus, the question of whether the cultural matrix exists at all is generally justified and relevant in the framework of this study. It is important in itself for understanding the relativity, imperfection, and non-universality of individual cultural matrices. This question confirms the important idea promoted in this book – a single national cultural matrix cannot claim to be the truth, it serves only as a tool to learn the truth.

CHAPTER 2

THE BELARUSIAN CULTURAL MATRIX

Roots of the Belarusian Cultural Matrix

Depending on the depth of analysis, one may identify different traits and similarities in the contemporary Belarusian cultural matrix.

On the surface of it, the Belarusian matrix seems to be similar to the Russian, Polish, Lithuanian, Ukrainian, and Jewish ones.[4344] At times, some regional traits of Russians and Europeans can be traced in Belarusians. Some elements of the Belarusian matrix are occasionally detected in international trends of the revival of traditional values in Russia, the national pride and communist values in China, the popular leadership in Indonesia, the spiritual authoritarianism in Africa, the folk pragmatism in the Philippines and Greece, the political charisma in the US, Turkey, and Hungary, the European nationalism, the Latin American populism, and the British conservatism.[45] The traits of the latter were already identified back in 1956, by Austrian economist Friedrich Hayek: "paternalistic, nationalistic, and power-adoring, … traditionalistic, anti-intellectual and often mystical".[46] Nowadays, it could be expressed as the well-known slogan "Make … Great Again"; just choose the name of the nation.

A deeper look at the Belarusian matrix would show that its traits go back to Soviet communism. Soviet ideological habits, and semi-conscious impulses, are the heavy legacy for the cultural matrix of Belarus. At least three traits of the Soviet man are deeply rooted, and appear in Belarusians of different generations.

1) Replacement of the individual 'I' with the sovereign 'we'. In this context, the sovereign 'we' does not mean public, and does not mean the sum of individuals. The sovereign 'we' is something ideological and symbolic. On the one hand, such a religious approach leads to fanaticism, a global mind-set, and orientation toward autocracy (which is even more pronounced among Russians). This results in thinking of one's exclusivity, incomparability, and unique path. On the other hand, it reveals an inverse dependence on the state and sovereign paternalism. As

a result, the Belarusian matrix is formed in the environment of constant contact with the state, and lack of understanding that one's life and partners could be different. Nevertheless, the individual 'I' has not completely disappeared; it is hidden at home. It results in indifference to anything that is beyond one's threshold: while one's home is kept tidy, there is disorganisation beyond its threshold, and that is addressed in an artificial (sovereign), rather than a natural (public) way.

2) Orientation to a system of bans rather than motivation to succeed. The mechanisms of motivation, competition among people, and leadership, were not developed in the USSR. The Soviet man was more likely to adapt to the repressive regime with a focus on simplification. Therefore, his main feature must have been the survival attitude. In this regard, the Soviet man looks rather cynical, hypocritical, unprincipled, not trusting the government, and concerned only with the issues of his own survival and wellbeing of his family and friends.[47] He clearly demonstrates 'the servant's trickery' combined with submissiveness, helpfulness, ignorance, and impudence. He relies on these features to demonstrate his primitive loyalty, while acting primarily to his own advantage. Such relations with the state are based on craftiness and playing the 'shell game' or 'cat and mouse'. At the same time, it is combined with ostentatious humbleness all the way down to subservience. It tells on one's appearance. American financial expert Michael Lewis notes that the communist heritage might be the reason why East Germans, for example, are more likely to slouch, while West Germans are much prouder and stand straight.[48]

3) Tactical rather than strategic mental models and behaviour. In the Soviet era, long ideological abstraction led to a low level of sensitivity of the public to long-term plans and strategies. In that context, the public became predisposed to concrete and immediate results. That is displayed in such features of modern Belarusians as, for example, their action for action's sake, search for quick solutions and satisfaction with foreseeable things, short planning horizons, and low propensity to invest replaced with high propensity to consume.

If one looks deeper into the darkness of Soviet communism, one can see creeping similarities to the extreme forms of the ideology of the past century – the Italian fascism and German Nazism. To some extent, these features echo in the modern Belarusian cultural matrix, in the part of traditionalism, irrationalism, quasi-activity, selective populism, patriarchy, and other things. The reader, however, may think that the case is overstated, with hardly observed similarities artificially dragged into focus and an extreme form of realism displayed. But this is done specifically to make one think, to prevent the transformation of sketchy similarities and potential risks to reality. Therefore, the signs of fascism, formulated by Italian philosopher Umberto Eco, should be still quoted:[49]

1) the cult of tradition;
2) the denial of modernity, irrationalism;
3) the cult of action for action's sake;
4) disagreement and doubt equal treason;
5) the fear of diversity, migrants, gays, xenophobia;
6) the appeal to the frustrated middle class;
7) the obsession with conspiracy theories;
8) pacifism is tantamount to fraternising with the enemy;
9) the weak are despised;
10) the cult of heroism and the cult of death;
11) selective populism. The nation is monolithic and its will is expressed by the supreme ruler;
12) masculinity, denial of substandard sexual behaviour;
13) lies and propaganda; and
14) the simplified newspeak preventing critical thinking.

In addition to certain similarities between communism and fascism, including their strong-arm methods of achieving goals, their differences are also visible. According to various sources, the differences between communism and fascism led most notably to the disappointment of many Germans in communist ideas in the 1920s-1930s, and their transition to Nazism.[50] Communism, unlike fascism, denies private property, social inequality of people, and the existence of classes, setting the goal of creating a socially homogeneous society. In its turn, fascism is built on the superiority of some nations over others, chauvinism, setting a final goal of creating a racially homogeneous society. The modern Belarusian society is, to some extent, socially and racially homogeneous. This society is undoubtedly far from communism and fascism, since it has become so in a natural rather than in an artificial way (although because of artificial developments); it has grown used to its current state, and this homogeneous atmosphere is already impacting the society and its values.

Going deeper into history to study the Belarusian matrix is of low practical value in the framework of this study, as this book is based on the hypothesis that social values are transmitted through social information channels rather than through biological or historical ones.

We are who we are mostly due to our information and cultural environment, rather than due to genetic factors or history. Therefore, there are natural limitations to the transmission of information in the form of social communication with living generations that form the structure of the Belarusian society and influence the surrounding cultural and information environment.

At the same time, historical studies of the Belarusian nation are of some interest. For instance, Belarusian culturologist Yulyia Chernyavskaya identifies three pillars of the common national idea of Belarusians: multiculturalism, the right to culture (cultural equality), and social equity.[51] These features, traced in Belarusians in the early part of the 20th century, are, to some extent, observed both earlier and later. Thus, it is asserted that some 'Soviet ethos' was ingrained in Belarusians long before the USSR times, while the Soviet values, especially 'land and equity', are the original values of any traditional society, which the Belarusian society also is. This seems to be fair, given that in the pre-Soviet period, Belarusians were mainly represented by rural residents carrying corresponding values. According to the census of 1897, only 17.1% of the population resided in cities and towns of Belarus.[52] It is noteworthy, that back in 1905, following his travels to the Belarusian region, Russian ethnographer Fedot Kudrinsky highlighted some similarities of the Belarusians to the Slavs, such as family-orientedness, kindness, and cordiality, as well as some distinctive features of the Belarusians, such as their uncertainty, gloominess, and silent diligence, that bears resemblance to contemporary Belarusians.[53]

But, plunging hastily into history to explain the contemporary Belarusian matrix often results in practical dissatisfaction and pessimism about the future. Historical search for similarities supports the social orientation to the past, and ultimately, to some extent, justifies the doom, predetermination, and hopelessness of the development of the Belarusian society. However, it is likely that some similarities between Belarusians' ancestors and contemporaries evidence only the common cultural and information environment that prevailed on the territory of Belarus in the early 20th and the 19th centuries. If one takes more remote examples of Rzeczpospolita, the Grand Duchy of Lithuania, and Ancient Rus, such similarities are lost, and what remains is only the desire of contemporaries to find a reference point in history, a role model to copy and formulate a modern national idea.

If we consider the Belarusian cultural matrix, not from the perspective of its historical roots, but through the theoretical lens, for example, within the framework of cultural studies (tabooing, ritualism, patterns, etc.), the contemporary position of Belarusian culturologist Irina Shumskaya is useful. She has divided the cultural matrix of Belarus into several key elements, which could be accepted, expanded, and supplemented.[54]

1) Tabooing the topic of death. "In Belarusian society, talking about death is considered almost rude by default, and the issue of the abolition of the death penalty is side-lined in every possible way in the public sphere".[55] The issue of the death penalty is associated with the way Belarusians appreciate justice, their undervaluation of human life (inherited from the Soviet days), isolated judgments, and a non-existent tradition of social dialogue to discuss key decisions being made. The taboo of the public discussion of the issue of death is combined with the veneration of ancestors — contemporary Belarusians respect the Christian days of commemoration of the departed (the 9th day, the 40th day, death anniversaries), and memorial days with pagan roots (Radunitsa, Dzyady). This dualism of the psyche and behaviour affirms such an important Belarusian trait as doublethink. In addition, the tangle of the veneration of ancestors, the mythical attitude toward death, and religious ritualism with elements of paganism affect the psyche, and form a certain inclination to believe in unreal things, prophetic dreams, reincarnation, and so on. In medical practice, this has its own explanation, which is associated with the human nervous system, rather than directly with the cultural matrix.[56]

2) Another example of tabooing is the positioning of power. The remaining large power distance results in tabooing the public discussion of the real incomes and expenses of government officials, openness of tax declarations of civil servants, and details of their career advancements. This leads to suspicion, association of power with high incomes, default public deprecation, and loss of confidence in government institutions. The distancing of power is one of the reasons for the ambivalent social orientation — that towards the Soviet past, or the uncertain future; towards the use of state symbols or the return to the Pursuit coat of arms and the white-red-white flag; towards Russia or the EU, and so on. This is also accompanied by an increasingly pronounced generation gap, and orientation based on the values of the older and the younger generations with some uncertainty in-between. The distancing of power is also combined with a clear understanding of the responsibility of the society for the country's social and economic development which characterises such a feature as sovereign paternalism. The distancing of power also

leads to increased costs of collective action, due to the transfer of social responsibility from society to the state, as well as to increased costs of doing business due to the transfer of economic responsibility from the business to the state.

3) Ritualism. It is the commemoration of memorable Soviet dates that supports the public orientation towards the Soviet past and the collective memory of the Great Patriotic War — March 8, May 1, May 9, June 22, July 3, November 7. At the same time, festive dates, monuments, and the names of streets and cities, hardly reflect the pre- and post-Soviet period of Belarusian history. In sum, this orientation towards the Soviet past maintains the focus on short-term planning, conditioned by the relatively short period of collective memory recorded in rituals.

4) Religious ritualism. During the period of June 2015 to July 2016, the Pew Research Centre conducted a survey of 18 countries (including Belarus), running face-to-face interviews with more than 25,000 people. The results of the survey show that 73% of interviewed Belarusians consider themselves to be Orthodox Christians, and 12% are Catholics. This is one of the highest ratios of Orthodox Christians to Catholics in Central and Eastern European countries. It is also reported that in Belarus, Catholics are more likely to go to church than Orthodox Christians — 25% of Catholics and 12% of Orthodox Christians go to church every week. At the same time, Catholics and Orthodox Christians are very tolerant towards each other — 73% of the Orthodox Christians are ready to accept Catholics as members of their families, just as 73% of Catholics are ready to welcome Orthodox Christians in theirs. In general, 84% of adult Belarusians report that they believe in God, while only 25% pray daily. It should be noted that, for example, in Poland, interviewed Poles can consider themselves 'true Poles' if they are Catholics, and Orthodox Christianity in Russia serves as a ground for interviewed Russians to be considered 'true Russians'. In Belarus, such a tangle of opinions about the national and the religious is observed in the case of 45% of respondents — one of the lowest indicators in countries with an Orthodox majority. In addition, only 42% of Belarusians believe that their culture is superior to all others.[57] Thus, although religious ritualism influences the cultural matrix of Belarus, it is not its determining factor.

5) Patterns – the language environment. An important feature of contemporary Belarusians is the way people use slang expressions.[58] The active use of criminal jargon, foul language, euphemisms, and the verbalisation of vulgarisms, is turning into the norm for communication, solving problems, conducting 'closed' meetings at the low and medium

levels, and 'comprehensible explanation' of complex problems. As such expressions are often used publicly, they become the social orientation, the trend, the norm for communication. According to the Independent Institute of Socio-Economic and Political Studies, only 6.5% of Belarusian citizens do not hear any abusive language at all, 23.4% hear it many times a day, 34.2% hear it daily, and 20.2% – several times a week. The specific linguistic atmosphere of Belarusian society could be rooted in the Soviet legacy of 'prison closeness'; the influence of modern Russian television with its popular crime TV series', the level of general education, the background of Belarusian public figures, and their place of residence.

As we can see from the above, the roots of the Belarusian cultural matrix maintain a specific cultural and information post-Soviet background or environment in the country, which affects the formation of modern features of the Belarusian cultural matrix.

The Belarusian Cultural Matrix: Features

In the framework of this study, the main features of the modern Belarusian matrix, which will be further empirically grounded, considered in more detail in the context of their effect on the economy, and subjected to decoding, include doublethink, orientation towards the Soviet past, and paternalism. They intertwine, forming other features and making the whole Belarusian matrix complex and unpredictable. The national cultural matrix covers the entire Belarusian society. It is reflected in every Belarusian organisation, group of people, family, and each individual Belarusian. On average, they are all alike within this cultural matrix, being influenced by it, and influencing it themselves.

Doublethink

Doublethink is a core feature of Belarusians. It is observed in reasoning, behaviour, simultaneous manifestation of two opposite features, and their rapid change. For instance, grumpiness and unsmilingness alternate with openheartedness, sternness and withdrawal – with charm and friendship, greed – with generosity, fear – with boldness, restraint – with improvisation, self-criticism – with inflated self-esteem, sentimentalism – with pragmatism, collectivism – with individualism, conservatism – with liberalism, authoritarianism – with democracy. To some extent, doublethink can be rendered tantamount to uncertainty, lack of self, shifting from one idea to another. The consistency of doublethink complicates Belarusians, making it possible to establish contact with them only at certain moments, when there is concurrence of ideas related to certain issues.

This feature of Belarusians could be largely explained by the legacy of Soviet doublethink, lack of clarity or definite self-identification, location at the borderline between the Russian and European regional cultural matrices, geopolitical uncertainty, contrasting information presented by state-sponsored and opposition media (for example, on TV or online), lingering economic transformation, and, although to a lesser extent, by bilingualism (the Russian and Belarusian languages) and religious dualism (Orthodox Christianity and Catholicism).

This is supported with the results of the survey conducted by the Pew Research Centre — doublethink is revealed in Belarusians' attitude towards the USSR, European and Russian values, and democracy. 54% of respondents view the collapse of the Soviet Union negatively, and 34% view it positively. However, the attitude of Belarusians to Mikhail Gorbachev (as a symbol of the collapse of the USSR) is better than to Joseph Stalin (as a symbol of the power of the USSR). For instance, 36% of Belarusians appreciated the historic role of Mikhail Gorbachev, while the positive role of Joseph Stalin was noted by only 26% of respondents. Regarding the choice between Russia and the West, 76% of respondents in Belarus believe that "strong Russia is necessary as a counterbalance to the influence of the West", and 56% fully and mostly agree that, "it is in the interests of our country to cooperate with the United States and other Western countries". There is no single-mindedness with respect to democracy either. For instance, 38% of respondents believe that "democracy is the best governance system", and 35% are certain that "in some circumstances, reliance on undemocratic practices might be better".[59]

Doublethink reflects the adaptation of the brain to uncertainty and instability. It affects decisions, making them unpredictable and inexplicable. They can be opposing, but convincing in both cases. There is a paradox. On the one hand, Belarusians manifest their confidence and firmness – "because I decided so", while on the other hand, they display their frustration and flexibility – "because nothing is decided". On the surface, this is expressed in such a national feature as "it doesn't matter ... it's good enough". In view of such to-and-fro motion, progress seems impossible. However, there is progress after all, and it becomes a subtle art – to hint in an ambivalent manner, to say without saying, to do without doing. It is a manifestation of subtlety, and development progresses in small, rope-walker, steps.

Doublethink splits and complicates such social features as collectivism and individualism, as well as emotionality and restraint. In this regard, Belarusians cannot be unambiguously characterised as being either the former or the latter. They simultaneously combine these traits, which swiftly alternate and are in constant dynamic equilibrium.

Collectivism and individualism. Collectivism in Belarus is formed under the influence of family-orientedness and Soviet legacy. The division into 'friends' and 'foes', natured by families, forms the Belarusian as a member of a small group, a small team. Nevertheless, at times, Belarusian collectivism unpredictably alternates with individualism, which contradicts collective interests. This Belarusian feature can be explained by limited mobility, and mental isolation. The individualism of Belarusians is often manifested spontaneously and uncontrollably, since there are no other social counterbalances, except for state ones, to adjust it for the benefit of the common collective good. The Belarusian individual is bright, charismatic, difficult to explain, being "in a world of one's own" – "because I decided so". Thus, Belarusians resemble a collection of dissociated units rather than a society. They are united by statehood rather than by common values and interests. At the same time, Belarusian individualism, bright though it is, should not be overestimated, since it is alleviated by doublethink. The Institute of Sociology of the National Academy of Sciences of Belarus compared the predisposition of Belarusians to the values of collectivism (stability, peace, comfort, support from others) with that to the values of individualism (initiative, enterprise, search for new things in life and work). The judgments of Belarusians appear to be practically midway, with a slight bias towards individualism. According to some other estimates, based on the databases of the European Social Survey, the World Values Survey, and Geert Hofstede's insights, Belarusians are more inclined to collectivism, albeit with a high proportion of individualism. 52.9% of Belarusians think that they are trying to help others, and 36.8% believe that they care only about themselves and their folks.

Emotionality and restraint. The emotionality of Belarusians is expressed through their charisma, they become familiar with strangers quickly, solving fundamental issues through personal trusting relationships. Such emotionality, along with sincerity and romantic idealism, is inherent in the Belarusians, as in all Slavs. Emotionality in decision-making is expressed through focusing more on external beauty than on internal convenience.

This is traced in the organisation of work, life, and choice of clothing. For example, Belarusian (Slavic) women give greater preference to fine dresses and high-heeled shoes than American or European women, who tend to choose comfortable jeans and sneakers. Another example is that houses in Belarus are built with the porch facing the street to 'profile oneself', while in China the porch faces the backyard, to be within 'one's circle'.

The Belarusian emotionality is combined with the impairment of social energy, expressed in restraint and tolerance. At times, Belarusians quickly make or change decisions according to emotions, intuition, and mood. At times, they are reserved and indecisive, indifferent and lazy, able to postpone their decisions. At times, they display some kind of provincial surrender to fate, or forbearance (*'pamiarkoŭnasć'*) traced through years of slowness and indecision, which is expressed in lack of punctuality, breach of agreements, and sometimes even in changing their opinions in the course of their own monologues. It is not uncommon for Belarusians to 'disappear', which is supposedly perceived as "internal work to reach an agreement". But, in fact, it is often just withdrawal, in the hope that the agreements will be reached by themselves – *'samo zrobićća'* (it will materialize by itself), or "the urgency and need will disappear". Mood swings, sudden and rapid shifts from emotionality to restraint and back, significantly complicate the perception of Belarusians of the surrounding world, and that of Belarusians by others. The dualism of emotionality and restraint is vividly expressed in stubborn striving to get the intended result, and then stopping almost at the very last moment and completely abandoning the plan. Culturologists state that the cultural and historical cause of this is found within the lives of people who could be deprived of everything at any moment in history.

Orientation to the Soviet Past

Along with doublethink, this is one of the most important roots of Belarusians. For most Belarusians, their history is limited to the Soviet period. According to a survey conducted in the spring of 2016, most Belarusians (68%) referred to the victory in the Great Patriotic War as the key historic event for Belarus. Among other milestones, Belarusians mentioned "the collapse of the USSR" (52%), "the Chernobyl Nuclear Power Plant accident" (45%), and "getting independence in 1991" (40%), while the remaining historic events got less than 30%.

This orientation to the Soviet past has taken root and is maintained in the Belarusian society through the state system, the memorial nature of the Great Patriotic War, family-orientedness, and the overall information environment. State military holidays, memorials to the Great Patriotic War, serve as a key reference point for Belarusians, which is somewhat weakened with the arrival of new generations. Back in 2013, sociological surveys showed that about 90% of Belarusians called the Great Patriotic War the main historic event for Belarusians, now their share is below 70%.[60] Partisan warfare, captivity, and being occupied, are important features of Belarusians' participation in the Great Patriotic War, which are imprinted in the collective memory. For example, according to Belarusian expert Valentin Akudovich, the partisan warfare of Belarusians during the war is a deep reflection of the "ontological substance of Belarusians": "a partisan is someone, who hides all the time ..., a partisan is someone, who keeps saying 'I do not exist', a partisan is someone, who comes to the light only at the moment of a sabotage attack and then disappears again to his non-existence".[61] Another example that characterises Belarusians during wartime was quoted by the Belarusian writer and Nobel prize winner for Literature, Svetlana Alexievich. When she once asked why there were fewer cases of the local population killing Jews in Belarus during the Second World War, she got the following response from eyewitnesses: "Yes, that was rare, but they could show for a sack of grain where they [Jews] were hiding...". In other words, it appears that Belarusians could do such things using others, and to their own profit. All these features are traced through generations.

In the modern Belarusian family, the older generation, which lived during the Soviet period, transmits Soviet values, stereotypes, and phobias, to the middle-aged generation, and the latter passes on the remains of such a legacy to the younger generation. In their turn, the Soviet symbols preserved in Belarus — names of streets, towns, and cities, holidays, monuments to Lenin and other Soviet leaders — reflect the unconscious orientation to the Soviet past, rather than an understanding of their meaning and conformity to contemporary values. The orientation to the Soviet past is one more root of Belarusian features such as orientation to scale and short-term results.

Orientation to scale. Large-scale thinking, inherited from a large country, results in geopolitical assessments and a national ideology of Belarusians which is not consistent with the reality of their own country, and its place and role in global, political, and economic, developments. In addition, Belarus' state institutions are either largely inherited from the Soviet past or rely on the needs of a centrally-managed state, which reinforces this orientation of the Belarusian society to scale. Such orientation is intertwined with the remains of Belarusians' Soviet pride which pushes the society to embed the Belarusian cultural matrix into the Russian regional matrix, which has inherited the Soviet cultural magnetism.

Orientation to short-term results. Orientation to short-term results, inherited from the Soviet days, is confirmed by sociological research. The survey of Belarusians, conducted by the Institute of Sociology of the National Academy of Sciences of Belarus in 2014, shows that most Belarusians are unable to share a long-term vision of their future. 37% of respondents state that they do not know what will happen to them, even in the coming months, and 25% of respondents are only able to foresee their life trends for the next year or two. 20% of respondents find it difficult to give any definite answer, only 10% of Belarusians can speak with confidence about their future for the next five to six years, and only 8% can predict many years to come.

Slow-down of time. Due to state involvement in public and personal life, people don't rush to make deals or implement decisions. They value time free from the state, coffee-breaks, lunch time, and holidays. All these are reflected in labour productivity. If a person manages to cheat the state and its norms, or use his personal motivation and informal links, then he may speed up time and increase his productivity. It was a normal way of working for the Soviet period of the 1970s, and the late 1980s.[62]

Paternalism

Along with doublethink and orientation to the past, this feature is the third root of the Belarusian matrix. Paternalism is ingrained in children by their families practically from the moment of their birth. Even the location of the crib next to parents, tight swaddling of babies, etc., are considered to have an impact.[63] In Belarus, this feature is reinforced by orientation to the Soviet past, combined with the remote decision-making centre, search for a support country, the 'big brother', and idealisation of the role of the individual in history. The historic choice was made after the collapse of the USSR, when the country faced a cultural dilemma: whether to build something understandable and appealing to people, something that corresponded to their culture, or something unknown and not reinforced by the public willingness to experiment. It could be the insufficient cultural ability of the society for sensible self-organisation and self-activity in this area that resulted in the movement towards centralisation and paternalism. A similar assessment of the post-Soviet period in Russia is offered by Russian economist Yevgeny Yasin.[64] It is noteworthy that the link between culture and democracy is often publicly claimed, and even declared. For example, in Sweden, it is reflected in the name of the relevant government body – the Ministry of Culture and Democracy.

Paternalism in Belarus gives a feeling of comfort, security, non-involvement, dependence, and passivity, with problems being solved by someone else. Understanding that the future does not depend on you, and cannot be changed, pushes you to live for the day. This, in turn, strengthens the orientation towards short-term results. In addition, paternalism weakens individual and public control, and transfers responsibility to the state represented by the leader, a certain government body, or its official. This creates an environment conducive not to independent actions, but to passive complaining. Paternalism in Belarus functions cyclically. Under the impact of doublethink, it strengthens to authoritarianism, sometimes up to frightening totalitarianism one day, easing off towards dirigisme, sometimes to ostensible liberalism, another day.

Authoritarianism and dirigisme. These two features can function independently, alternating in an unpredictable way, but always remaining within the framework of paternalism. At the same time, both paternalism, and its forms of authoritarianism and dirigisme, cannot be limited only to the system of public administration. Although certain studies sometimes classify the Belarusian authoritarianism specifically as that of the state, associating it with the experience of other countries 'stuck in the transformation' (Albania, Haiti, Guyana, Madagascar, Malaysia, Russia, Tanzania, and others),[65] this feature is inherent, and manifested in the whole Belarusian cultural matrix, and is, therefore, characteristic of each Belarusian in varying degrees.

Strengthening paternalism to authoritarianism creates a mechanism for producing 'carbon-copy' people with similar mentality and behaviour. That creates a mirror universe. The willingness of subordinates to guess the solution convenient for a manager leads to moving in circles, with no fresh ideas promoting progress allowed. The extreme centralisation of decision-making, while it is physically impossible to digest all the necessary information, results in lower quality decisions. At the same time, it establishes a monopoly over the information of critical importance to all, the loss of which could become a general catastrophe. There are many historic examples, when the centralisation of information and decision-making at the most senior government level led to managerial errors in time of peace, military losses in time of war, and a tragedy for the whole community. The obvious example of that is the experience of fascist Germany, taken both in general, and in particular, cases. One well-known example is when Hitler literally slept through the clearance of the order repelling the landing of allied forces in Normandy, and no one dared to wake him, although German tank forces were near the landing site and could have extinguished the attack.

Authoritarianism is successfully preserved in an isolated society. But, the increasing awareness of the population warms up its expectations, and new questions and needs arise faster than they can be satisfied by the authoritarian regime. This results in a mental gap between the public and the authorities. Expectations of a better future are visualised, and hopes emerge that "tomorrow life should be better than yesterday" and, moreover, that "tomorrow life should be as good as that of others, or even better". This creates prerequisites for the obvious inability of authoritarianism to meet such needs as freedom, self-expression, and political representation. The lack of ideological power of authoritarianism to influence informed, self-sufficient, and independent people results in a manifestation of its monopoly right to violence, and the use of harsh measures of social coercion. In this case, various forms of repressive measures are possible: from mass ones, such as in the early years of the totalitarian regime in the Soviet Union, to selective ones, such as at a later stage of authoritarianism in the USSR. Under the pressure of forceful actions, the public develops 'Stockholm Syndrome' – the empathy and alliance of the hostage, who is waiting to regain his right to violence. In turn, when the feeling of self-righteousness of the agencies executing the forceful actions diminishes, the repressive mechanism weakens, creating an amorphous environment of mutual inaction.

The stability of authoritarianism over time, strangely enough, depends on its own actions and mistakes rather than on external influence or internal opposition. Excessive self-confidence and misrepresentation of information heighten the risk of getting into difficulties and prevents the summoning up of the necessary strength or forming a vision of how to address them.[66] Nevertheless, authoritarianism is sometimes saved thanks to doublethink, the ability to take a softer form in time, to take half a step back into dirigisme, and then returning to its usual averaged state of paternalism.

The roots and features considered above are similar, and, at the same time dissimilar, to the modern cultural matrix of Belarus, which seems simultaneously Soviet and not Soviet, Russian and not Russian, European and not European. This impression is created as the Belarusian matrix, as well as the whole country, is transformational. And this is its essence. It is unstable and changeable. It is mesmerised by constant movement. It moves forward to new, unknown, individual, and multicultural things one day, then gets frightened of the unknown and reverts to the comfortable circle of trust, the silent environment of waiting. This transitional state of the Belarusian matrix has become permanent over the years, has formed a relatively stable institutional environment, and stopped between the two extremes.

The features and comparisons of the Belarusian matrix offered here are visible clearly and fully when viewed from outside, from another country, a different matrix. It should be taken into account that the view of an outsider can be distorted by the different cultural matrix, which serves as a basis for benchmarking cultural values. The idealisation of American, European, Chinese, and other values often leads to pessimism and deliberate criticism of the cultural matrix of Belarus. Such an alarming view of the Belarusian matrix is exacerbated by protracted problems in the country's economy. Thus, the economy often facilitates making a fairly accurate assessment of the cultural matrix, its efficiency and impact on the society. It is the level of wellbeing of the population that can serve as an indicator, a common denominator for assessing cultural matrices of different countries. It helps determine the cultural environment that is most conducive to business, economic development, and people's lives. Moreover, when living standards deteriorate and prospects of economic development weaken, similar values, priorities, and tasks are shared by people of different cultural matrices, races, and faiths. The same happens at a high level of economic development, when representatives of different cultural matrices develop common interests, views, and values. All this suggests that the economy can be, and is, only one — albeit an essential — part of our life.

CHAPTER 3

"BECAUSE I DECIDED SO"

"Why do reforms fail in Belarus?" "Why don't we need economists?" These questions were raised in Belarusian economic forums in 2016, 2015, and before, and remain relevant today. There is one short answer to them: "Because I decided so".

This is the answer the average Belarusian would give. Such answers add up to "Because we decided so". Then, this total is delegated, in the form of powers to those who make final decisions in the economy at the level of households, enterprises, holdings, industries, sectors, and the country. As a result, 'we' transforms back into "Because I decided so". All these individual, collective, and again individual, decisions are closely interconnected. Sometimes they mirror each other, and often try to divide responsibility. But the responsibility which is triggered by the first individual decision is shared. If every Belarusian made a different decision, the behavioural economics and answers to the questions about reforms and economists would be different. However, here, in the framework of this study, the focus is different – not on 'what' decision is made, but on 'how' it is made. It is not on whether the right or wrong decision is made, but on how it is made, which socio-cultural factors affect it, what stands behind it, which values and which cultural matrix form its basis, and how this matrix affects the economy, what vision of the economy and behaviour it develops in Belarus.

For the purposes of this book, I approach the study of the cultural matrix and its effect on the economy from two perspectives. On the one hand, I rely on expert appraisals; opinions based on theory, Belarusian and international practices, historical evidences, our own appraisals, impressions, intuition, and personal experiences of being inside and outside the Belarusian cultural matrix. On the other hand, I resort to sociological surveys, an attempt to understand the confessions of Belarusians, their visions, embellishment, desires, expectations, fears, and lies.

This chapter presents an expert appraisal of the Belarusian cultural matrix and its effect on the Belarusian economy. How are the national psyche and behaviour reflected in the economy? What stands behind the phrase "Because I decided so"? Answers to these questions would make it possible to examine the structure of the behavioural economics of Belarus in detail, and see all its complexity and inconsistency.

Doublethink

Doublethink is reflected in the Belarusian economy in the following areas.

A mix of administrative and market relations. As there are no checks and balances in the form of fully-fledged market institutions, the economy is still characterised by administrative permissiveness, which is influenced by the Belarusian doublethink. For instance, in the context of the underdeveloped financial market, the estimated cost of investment and allocation of financial resources is unpredictable: "it could cost so much or so much", "money might be allocated to this or that". Another example is the monetary sphere, where the declared market orientation (the freely floating exchange rate, inflation targeting, market pricing) is combined with currency restrictions, partly administratively regulated prices of goods and interest rates, the still administrative management of resources, projects, enterprises, industries, and the whole economy. This is reflected in the way inflation is registered. It has been divided into two parts for a long time – the core index, which covers the monetary factor, net of administrative regulation and seasonal price fluctuations, and the administratively regulated index, which covers indirect taxes, utilities, and so on.

Inconsistent and contradictory economic policies. Doublethink leads to the inconsistent implementation of a number of reforms. For example, the implementation of the 2016 redenomination in the context of the double-digit inflation — it was 16.2% in 2014, 12% in 2015, and 10.6% in 2016 – – and unreformed corporate and social sectors. At the same time, reforms in the utilities sector, whether gradual or decisive, the inevitable elimination of cross-subsidisation, reduction of government programme financing, shedding of state-owned enterprises' non-core assets, etc., would, in any case, result in some pertinent consumer inflation. In this regard, it is logical to start the implementation of economic reforms with the real, rather than the financial, sector. That would promote an inflow of liquid foreign exchange resources to bring reserves to the safe level needed to instil the exchange and financial stability.

Inconsistencies in forms of ownership and management systems. Belarusian society demonstrates an ambivalent attitude to ownership. On the one hand, large state-owned enterprises are perceived by Belarusians as national symbols, which should not be privatised. On the other hand, since there were no proprietary rights in Soviet times, the right of ownership of apartments and cars has gained primary value, and is, at times, unconsciously perceived as an apparent freedom. In addition, there is inexplicable doublethink in Belarus, where, for instance, the machine building and petrochemical sectors, light industry, and telecommunications, are state-owned, while the military-industrial complex, banking system, IT sphere, retail trade, and real estate are privately owned. Enterprises, in which the state holds 50% + 1 share, account for a fairly stable share of the Belarusian GDP – 47-49% in 2011-2016. Whereas, the GDP share attributed to enterprises, in which the state holds 50% or less, was 51-53%. The mix of different forms of ownership leads to the juxtaposition of different management systems. In this case, the private sector also demonstrates its doublethink, trying to adapt to the state to get an opportunity to benefit from government support, budget programmes, and state guarantees. In their turn, state-owned enterprises in Belarus, given the export orientation of the Belarusian economy and its dependence on imports, must invariably cooperate with foreign, normally private companies. It reinforces the doublethink in the economic psyche of Belarusian state-owned enterprises and encourages them to act differently: "It could be done this way or that way, but it's best to pick something in-between".

A mix of ostentatious loyalty and pursuit of personal interests. The 'theatrical' loyalty to state ownership, as well as to the government institutions and legislation associated with it, is sometimes mixed with the unfailing pursuit of personal interests. Such doublethink is manifested in self-limitation combined with permissiveness. This leads to economic crimes, shadow transactions, and corruption. According to various estimates by Belstat and the World Bank, the share of the shadow economy in Belarus ranges from 9% to 50%. The estimate of about 35-37% offered by the National Academy of Sciences of Belarus and Belarusian State Economic University seems more realistic. But, it is alarming that this indicator is growing — it was 28% in 2002, 35% in 2012, and by 2020 it is projected to reach 40%. That is combined with a growing number of discovered economic crimes, sham companies, an amount of damage, and imposed penalties. The defensive reaction of enterprises trying to fight that, especially in the state-owned sector, is sabotage, go-slow strikes, hack-work, and use of complex incompatible tools and half measures aimed at preserving the existing habitual ambivalence. As a result, in the context of the officially registered economic recession, the economy continues to grow, although already at a different pace, in its shadow, beyond the framework of statistical records.

Ambiguous concepts and negotiations. Definitions are sometimes obviously ambiguous, while instructions and rules based thereon are unrealisable. In some cases, the same word, 'instruction', or 'task', may have an opposite meaning, or be differently understood by those issuing an instruction and those implementing it, which leads to definitely distorted performance. In turn, this gives room for maneuver to manipulate decisions, or to discover some hidden sense to one's benefit. Within the economy, it becomes common sense to fail to abide by agreements or legislation, or to disengage from obligations if, at some point, they become unfair or disadvantageous. At the same time, the abandonment of obligations does not lead to 'losing face', because it is considered correct, logical, and fair. Otherwise, if these conditions are met, obligations are strictly implemented, sometimes even at a loss. A 'double game' in negotiations allows for misdirection and the achievement of short-term results. But in the long run, it builds an ambiguous reputation, reduces credibility, and creates uncertainty and risks of disorientation and instability.

Collectivism and Individualism

In his study, based on the data collected by Dutch sociologist Geert Hofstede, and covering some 30 countries, Yuriy Gorodnichenko, Professor of Economics at Berkeley, argues that, of all the dimensions of culture, collectivism-individualism, or rather individualism, matters most for long-run economic growth.[67] Its influence on growth is channelled through innovations that are rewarded most in an individualist society. Moreover, this influence even off-sets the negative effect of undeveloped institutions on economic growth.[68] In another study, he finds that a social trait such as individualism contributes more than collectivism to the adoption of democracy in a country.[69]

As noted above, collectivism in Belarus is explained by the Soviet legacy, a traditionally relatively low level of urbanisation, family-orientedness, and lack of experience of historically transmitted classical democracy. Taken together, these factors form a narrow circle of trust, where collectivism extends to one's own group rather than to the whole society, which is reflected in the economic behaviour of Belarusians. To name a few examples, they prefer to borrow from acquaintances, hold money at home, do business with schoolmates. The deeply rooted family-orientedness, for instance, makes it highly likely that relatives and acquaintances may come to a person who has improved his income and social status, for financial help and social support. As a result, Belarus has a limited range of external partners, with creditors, investors, and trade counterparts from Russia, and from other mentally similar countries dominating this group. In turn, Belarusians treat 'outsiders', or foreigners, with curiosity and suspicion, sometimes combined with an aspiration to deceive them. Therefore, the consumer attitude in Belarus is often the most prominent feature noted by foreign investors, who often respond by characterising Belarusians as 'greedy', since "they focus only on consumption".

At the macro level, collectivism in the Belarusian economy is manifested in the perception of the wellbeing of the state as the wellbeing of the 'people', or some abstract society, rather than a multitude of concrete people. Therefore, the task of the state is to ensure economic growth rather than to grant freedom to independently improve one's living standards. A man's social values are formed top-down, brought to his notice, and perceived by him as his own. For example, the Soviet norm that sovereign, collective, interests should prevail over individual ones, is still maintained. There is a persistent imbalance – too much sovereign (but not public) 'we' and too little 'I'. Thus, at the micro level, individual entrepreneurs, and small and medium-sized businesses, are often mentally opposed to state-owned enterprises with large collectives. This creates conditions for unfair competition between the state-owned and the private sectors, for lobbyism and paternalism, the distorted allocation of financial and labor resources, and unequal access to government support and programmes.

Collectivism in Belarus is combined with individualism. Belarusians' individualism is specific. It manifests itself suddenly in making and implementing one's own decisions — and it is most important that these decisions are one's own. Such individualism, shaped in "because I decided so," is manifested in a commitment to principles, emphasis on a single, sometimes insignificant, detail that overrides collective interests. Individualism results in pettiness, provinciality, barriers to cultural diffusion, formation of one's own strange outlook, fantasising, belief in unbelievable things, and conspiracy. In view of that, the Belarusian society looks like a community of independent unpredictable units – 'black swans', which collectively, and sometimes unconsciously, impact the economy. This concept of the 'black swan', which is popularised in a book by an American economist, Nassim Nicholas Taleb, means the emergence of unpredictable and rare events with universal, significant, consequences.[70]

Individualism in the Belarusian economy pushes the individual to remain enclosed within his territory. It makes land a priority factor of production, due to limited mobility. This is probably the reason why agriculture becomes, mentally, the most comfortable area of activity, and economic policies of import substitution seem to be natural and logical. In turn, emotional neutrality and indifference manifest themselves in an attitude towards new, 'abstract' industries, such as finance and ICT. Loss of communication with the world, and remaining locked within one's own outlook, lead to readiness to break one's obligations. It justifies revisions of contractual relations, reduces the propensity for long-term investments, and strengthens the orientation towards short-term results. Thus, since Soviet times, loans, for example, are perceived not as repayable investments, which should generate returns, but rather as support that "we will repay somehow", and "maybe we will not need to repay". Therefore, under the influence of individualism, economic decisions become impulsive and short-term, and introduce uncertainty, while economic policies leaning towards isolation and traditional industries constrain the transformation of the economy.

Emotionality and Restraint

Emotionality promotes enthusiasm, energy, and dynamism, which are vital for the economy. It manifests itself in negotiations and meetings which are the main form of economic decision-making. At the same time, it is their own understanding of justice and equality, rather than wellbeing, profit, or money, that can become the determinant of Belarusians' decision-making. However, emotional satisfaction can be achieved not because 'you feel better', but because the competitor, the partner, the neighbor feels 'worse'. In the process of business negotiations, there is general friendliness and a focus on results. But if some injustice is detected, an explosive, extremely sharp, emotional reaction, sometimes disproportionate to the problem, is possible. Aggressive behaviour is often justified by one being treated unequally. When one feels right and strong, he might resort to theatrical rudeness, and even impudence, which gives a false sense of equality.

The atmosphere of business negotiations and the business climate are determined by emotion, rather than by their contents. The tone and intonation of speech are more important than the direct meaning of transmitted words. In negotiations, deep analysis can rarely be traced, and actions are often spontaneous, taken on the spur of the moment, depending on the circumstances, and based on the rule "we get involved first and then we'll see". Under the influence of emotion, a decision may be changed by a different, new, approach to addressing the old problem. Certain compromises arise, creating a feeling that the issue is unfinished, unresolved, and cannot ultimately be solved.

Belarusians rarely listen attentively to what their counterparts are saying, often thinking their position over in parallel. They can interrupt the interlocutor if they have formulated their opinion and are ready to present it. When dealing with sensitive topics, they quickly build close personal relationships, involving self-analysis and criticism of others. It is noteworthy that such personal relationships and sympathies sometimes contribute to the solution of seemingly deadlock issues. This is explained by the fact that a Belarusian is a person belonging to a small group.

The emotionality of Belarusians is often accompanied and balanced by another feature – restraint, or tolerance. Restraint can exist independently of emotion for a long time. If seen positively, restraint looks like judiciousness, discipline, or weighted decision-making based on life experience. It would seem to be the potential source of growth in labor productivity, and of the whole economy. But, on the other hand, restraint is imprinted on the faces of Belarusians as apathy, despondency, pessimism, and anger, which creates prerequisites for economic depression. Tolerance characterises the feeling of suppressed energy, learned helplessness, and despair. Sometimes there is a sense of living in vain, a weak belief in the future, a lack of things to be proud of. This environment promotes short-term planning, and unnecessarily excessive consumption, based on the principle that "we only get one shot at life", "we live for the day", and "payday to payday", which leads to consumer lending for knowingly unprofitable purposes – vacations, housing repair, cars, apartments. All that stretches this feature to the utmost, leading to depression bordering on aggression, which threatens the internal and social equilibrium. To release their emotions and ensure self-realisation, Belarusians demonstrate fussy pseudo-activity and self-destructive behaviour, sometimes expressed in being more prone to alcoholism, drug addiction, gambling, and suicide.[71]

In the economic context, it is possible to explain the restraint of Belarusians in different ways. As discussed above, restraint is an imprint of the Soviet legacy. Belarusian Nobel prize winner for Literature, Svetlana Alexievich, notes that the long-standing belief in communism has programmed self-sacrifice, the karma of suffering and tolerance.[72]

The tolerance of Belarusians is also affected by the fear of the tragedy of the Second World War, the collapse of the USSR, and examples of armed conflicts in neighbouring countries (Russia, Ukraine). In addition, a certain historical legacy also prevails, as the Belarusian territory, passed from hand to hand for many centuries, was the place of religious change, and the battle ground of the Russian-Polish, and other wars. All these factors have contributed to the low level of economic expectations and the perception of the economic reality: "it could be worse", "as long as there is no war". At the same time, under the influence of doublethink, Belarusians mix concepts and features. As a result, there are irrational associations which are not confirmed by history or modern practice; that, for example, war is practically the price of economic growth, or that economic reforms inevitably lead to war.

To some extent, the restraint of Belarusians and the influence of this on the economy can also be explained by the ecological environment. The cold climate, few sunny days, remoteness from the sea, and a meat-based diet form the so-called 'Nordic restraint'. A number of studies, covering 26 countries over the period from 1982 to 1997, as well as New York over the period from 1927 to 1990, have found a correlation between investment activity, average stock prices, and the number of sunny days (the studies also confirm a correlation between the size of tips given to waiters and the weather).[73] In turn, people's nutrition (especially in childhood), and the vitamin content of their diet, affect growth, weight, mind (IQ level), success, and wellbeing, as well as emotionality, which is characterised by a sense of happiness.[74] However, the experience of neighboring countries, and countries with a similar climate, such as Lithuania, Estonia, Latvia, Norway, Denmark, and Sweden, reminds us that we should take the impact of the climate factor on the economy into account, but not overestimate it.

Orientation to the Soviet Past

In Belarus, the legacy of the Soviet (Stalin) model of the mobilisation economy with limited business and civic activity reinforces the high propensity of economic agents towards passivity and paternalism. The orientation towards the Soviet past in the Belarusian economy creates a specific business climate, which can be described figuratively as a 'storage cage'. It is focused on preserving – sometimes through the use of force – the inherited management system, the decision-making mechanism, state ownership, and economic structure. The reliance on the Soviet ideology – – which has not been replaced in Belarus with anything else after the collapse of the USSR — and on its individual elements, generates some internal comfort, self-confidence, conviction about the legitimacy of management, and economic decisions.

The preserved Soviet management system instils a natural selection of loyal, closed-minded, predictable people, who are 'designed' to carry out assignments. This creates an atmosphere of conservative solidarity, and dissatisfaction with the future in the state apparatus, which limits experiments, risks, and innovations. In this environment, the administrative apparatus is motivated by threats and fear, and the main stake is on 'securocrats'; secret service, intelligence agency officers. They are officials too, but they are more disciplined, easier to manage, and more patriotic. Since, by virtue of their profession, they are more often faced with the mental opposition of 'friends' and 'foes', patriotism becomes more deeply rooted in them at the departmental level. They are persistently recruited into the management system that supports the Soviet tradition of negative incentives.

As a result, a self-sufficient, repressive, legal system is built up, and operates in the environment of its own arbitrary logic of patriotism – preserving the existing political and socio-economic relations. Sometimes it masks commercial interests. In this atmosphere of abuse of power and fear, anyone, including confidants and supervisors themselves, can become a victim of chaotic violence, which calls for stronger public control. All this reduces mutual trust and mutual respect, since such a system appeals to instincts rather than to reason. Instincts suppress the initiative and will, and do not give the expected result. In the atmosphere of fear, administrators are in a constant state of stress, and address only current tasks, for which they are held accountable here and now. This stress is a barrier to making rational, long-term decisions, it leads to persistent depression, burnout, and lower labour productivity. Such a system of control is comfortable and safe for the authorities, since the administrative apparatus is wrestling with itself, in extreme cases – to gain influence rather than change the regime.

The Soviet decision-making mechanism used in Belarus relies on a mix of personal informal arrangements and their written formalisation – "It is better to put everything in writing, sign, and set a seal". Written agreements give confidence that they will be realised, although in practice they are often followed only temporarily, and so long as they bring benefits. In decision-making, the Soviet logic of simple choice by contradiction is developed: "it should be done this way or no way", "if this social system is dismantled, there will be unemployment and poverty", "if it is not state-owned, it will be no one's and will be lost". The latter partially explains the remaining high share of state ownership in Belarus.

Even despite their corporatisation, state-owned enterprises created in the times of the USSR continue to exist in Belarus with no actual change of owner. Their operational and financial management has been intertwined with public administration ever since Soviet times. Ministries are *de facto* responsible for solving the problems of their subordinate enterprises, while the state budget is responsible for their financial condition. And conversely, if a state-owned enterprise is successful, its head can aspire to the position of the minister, and the company is to make extra transfers to the budget, in addition to taxes and dividends. Thus, it solves problems of the government, and conceals the mistakes of government fiscal and economic policies.

In the case of privatisation of state-owned enterprises, the risk of their re-nationalisation remains. This risk is treated as an opportunity to restore 'popular justice', since the population sees state-owned enterprises as public ones. It is noteworthy that, in many respects due to this public attitude, such expressions as 'privatisation', and 'selling an enterprise to an investor' are replaced in bureaucratese with 'attracting an investor'. This attitude is further reinforced by the unsuccessful experience of privatisation in Russia and Ukraine in the 1990s. It is important though, to consider the mistakes of these countries in privatisation: the preservation of monopolies, inconsistency of privatisation and nationalisation, lack of alignment with other economic reforms, gratuitous transfer of state-owned enterprises, lack of plans for their modernisation, corruption, and conflict of interests when civil servants are also members of the management of state corporations.[75] In practice, these errors were taken into account, say by Estonia, which managed to avoid monopolisation of privatised state-owned enterprises and improve its performance.

It should be specifically noted, that there is one more important reason for the preservation of state ownership in Belarus. It is the Soviet perception of power through the ownership and centralised management of large state-owned enterprises. However, this way of thinking does not agree with the modern system of values, when the combination of power and ownership is perceived as corruption, and these are start-ups rather than 'national champions' that generate the greatest value for society. Moreover, in the modern world, real power is no longer concentrated in enterprises with large collectives, it is dispersed in cyberspace.

This typical attitude to state-owned property in Belarus does not preclude its privatisation, which first takes the form of transformation of state-owned enterprises into open joint-stock companies (OJSC), followed by their sale. In 2011-2016, 344 Belarusian state-owned enterprises were transformed into OJSCs, with shares of 12 of those sold partially to foreign investors for a total of USD 2.5 billion. All in all, 5,150 state-owned enterprises were reformed in the period of 1991 to 2016. Some of them were sold to foreign investors at a fairly high price. The largest privatisation transactions in Belarus include:

1) The (staged) sale of a 100% stake in *Beltransgaz* OJSC for a total of USD 5 billion, a 31% stake in the statutory fund;
2) *Mobile Digital Communications* JV LLC – for USD 556 million, 80% of shares;
3) *Belarusian Telecommunications Network* CJSC – for USD 500 million, 93.27% of shares;
4) *Belpromstroibank* OJSC – for USD 280.7 million.

These examples demonstrate the doublethink, selective, approach to state-owned property, and the impact of factors which are sometimes unknown and not understandable to all, on decision-making.

The proneness towards the Soviet past weakens the orientation of Belarusian society towards building its future, which seems dangerous, since it is unknown. This restrains the structural modernisation of the Belarusian economy. But sources of financing are needed to maintain the familiar structure of the Belarusian economy, in the context of the slow development of its new elements and increasing deceleration of the old ones. In recent years, with the fall of exports — USD 51.8 billion in 2012, USD 29.8 billion in 2016 — and outflow of foreign direct investments —

USD 6.6 billion accumulated in 2014 and USD 6.4 billion in 2016 — the only way to maintain the traditional structure of the Belarusian economy would be borrowing.

As there were no external loans mobilised from the IMF and international financial markets during the economic crisis of 2015-2016, the domestic debt began to grow. Over the two years, it grew from USD 4 billion as at January 1 2015, to USD 5.2 billion as at January 1 2017. That did not bring economic recovery though — the real GDP growth was negative 3.8% in 2015, and negative 2.6% in 2016. Moreover, it began to deplete internal reserves and bring down real incomes — by 7.3% in 2016 — and savings of households. In 2016, for the first time ever, household deposits began to drop, especially in foreign currency. Thus, orientation towards the Soviet past started to turn into a factor contributing to the declining wellbeing of the population.

Orientation to Scale

This Belarusian feature is derived from the orientation towards the Soviet past. The preserved economic structure, management system, and other Soviet attributes, project a scale of economic thinking and behaviour that is incomparable with the national reality of Belarus. In Soviet times, this made sense in the context of ideological, physical, and information isolation. At that time, orientation to scale fitted the format of government planning, concentration of resources, and their directed allocation. At present, decentralised systems are becoming more effective in the context of openness. It is easier and cheaper to attract resources (money, goods, services, people, information) than to create them domestically. At the same time, the orientation to scale inherited by Belarus forms the propensity to produce almost everything to ensure self-sufficiency and implement large-scale full-production-cycle projects. But the full production cycle comes down, in practice, to final assembly, with low added value generated and only the appearance of integrity preserved. Orientation towards the production of everything leads to distorted forms of import substitution – this could be compared to a worker who tries to make an improvised car himself.

The habit of large-scale thinking also generates false expectations of large innovations, which normally depend on the market capacity, and are unlikely in Belarus. At the same time, there is no denying that Belarusians are ingenious, creative, and inventive. But that is a fragmentary and forced solution to untypical tasks, for instance when one has to perform the functions of a joiner, driver, cleaner, gardener, cook, educator, doctor, lawyer, accountant, etc. The attempt to embrace everything at a time is usually a solution to the challenge of surviving here and now. It is caused by low incomes and poor development of the relevant market segments and institutions, rather than the propensity to innovate. Under this approach, Belarusians undertake responsibility for all spheres of life, although it is difficult to become an expert in everything without proper training in all these areas. That leads to fussiness, pettiness, and fatigue. The time needed to recover, reflect, and make informed long-term decisions, is wasted. In this environment, the government apparatus oriented to scale becomes congested and inefficient, while officials either have nothing to lose, or focus on solving their own problems. At the same time, the orientation of management to scale sometimes masks such motives as the sense of power, its concentration and retention, patronage, corruption, etc.

Orientation to Short-Term Results

The orientation of Belarusians to short-term results can be explained in the following way. First, the horizon of planning the future largely depends on the range of collective memory of the past. Orientation towards the Soviet past, combined with orientation towards the period of life expectancy, predetermines short-term planning. Secondly, the technological boost, sharp fluctuations in the financial and commodity markets, and political unpredictability observed in recent years, stir up skepticism about long-term strategies and a transition to more frequent monitoring of the situation, with short-term control of results. Management looks like a firefighting team, and tight deadlines create tunneling.

In the Belarusian economy, orientation towards short-term, visible, results has long been regarded as effective policy. The economic and industry ministers think of themselves as fast problem-solvers. Sometimes they pay for one thing, while hoping for another. They ask both for speed and quality. However this is not easy to achieve. Although the solution looks attractive through the tunnel, savings today create greater expenses in the future. The decision-makers tend to neglect important, but not urgent, tasks. Sendhill Mullainathan, and Eldar Shafir, call this the 'scarcity trap' in their bright book, *Scarcity*.[76] They explain such a mindset and behaviour not through inherited social traditions, but a poor economic environment.

In the 1990s and 2000s, a compilation of short-term results (GDP growth, real incomes, and average wages raise, construction of facilities) created a sense of long-term economic stability in Belarus. In the 2010s, the slowdown and drop in economic growth demonstrated that long-term economic growth is not a string of hundred-metre races, but a marathon. The proof of this was the mounting inflationary and debt overhang – the chronic inability to reach an inflation rate of 2-3%, and the rate of government debt growth exceeding the rate of economic growth.

It is noteworthy that short-term tricks in the financial sphere continue to preserve the appearance of economic stability in Belarus. But this is a random element of luck, rather than conscious economic policy. Unlike the long-term orientation of the society, which encourages maximisation of profits, the short-term orientation leads to a propensity to minimise losses. Thus, the short-term orientation develops a greater propensity of the population to consume rather than to save and invest. This reduces the potential for long-term economic growth, and pushes the inflation up. In addition, the orientation towards quick results limits the curiosity that generates innovation, which also has a negative effect on the economy.

Orientation towards short-term planning creates the main incentive in the economic management system, i.e., reporting on the execution of the current task, such as preparing for a specific meeting, a visit, or a report. It generates some centralised short-term dynamism, which contributes to the atmosphere of visibility of results, and, therefore, the effectiveness of such policies. The goal is to get a quick and significant result by implementing short-term solutions. It is expected that, in the long run, if a problem arises, a short-term solution will be found again. Short-term planning is also well-aligned with the desire to keep the situation under control, rather than let it go, yielding to the incognisable complexity of individual incentives and hoping for their self-organisation. It is noteworthy that even political stability, which in theory should form strategic thinking and long-term responsibility, moving away from the solution of immediate problems, does not help overcome such a strong Belarusian feature.

Paternalism

In the best-case scenario, paternalism in the economy does a good deed, as the state provides services that individuals cannot organise themselves. Moreover, such services are usually expensive. There are no other unambiguously verifiable economic merits of paternalism. The years-long growth of the Belarusian economy was accompanied by the growth of commodity markets (oil, potassium) and the Russian market, and inflow of foreign capital to Belarus, not unlike in other developing countries. With the fall of these markets and a change in the direction of international capital flows, the Belarusian economy faced a recession.

To take one example, the average annual Brent oil price per barrel was USD 111.26 in 2011, USD 111.63 in 2012, USD 108.56 in 2013, USD 98.97 in 2014, USD 52.32 in 2015, and USD 43.55 in 2016. As a result, the foreign exchange earnings from oil exports dropped by USD 6.4 billion in 2015-2016. Thus, it's not paternalism, it's luck; a fortuitous combination of circumstances.

In the context of paternalism, however, the public blames it for everything. Dissatisfaction with paternalism comes about when it replaces market self-regulation, but is unable to provide the standard of living anticipated by the public. Or, when the public feels the urge to be treated by the state as an equal. The unpreparedness and unwillingness of the public to resist paternalism leads to emotional social discontent. The latter is usually expressed in passive anticipation of one paternalism being replaced by some other, rather than in active resistance and creation of a different system – pluralism with collective management and responsibility.

When paternalism is under threat because of, say, economic problems, it finds it rational to attract technocrats. For instance, a while back Chile engaged economists from Chicago – the Chicago boys.[77] Indonesia relied on the Berkeley Mafia, and Argentina, China, Malaysia, Singapore, and Taiwan engaged experts from international financial organisations, renowned economists, and famous representatives of the diaspora.[78]

In Belarus, the government plays the role of the technocrats. However, their proposals are not unique, and not final. Several technical views, down to the layman's opinion, are generated in the process of decision-making, which allows them to be thrown together offering the choice as to the one that will preserve paternalism. As a result, the government makes a mainstream decision to preserve the status quo, or find a compromise which is unpredictable and difficult to comprehend. This is how the premise "because I decided so" is generated; it lifts the responsibility from technocrats and simultaneously creates uncertainty. It disorientates, distorts incentives, and leads to false investments, and, ultimately, chaos. At the same time, technocrats still hope that they will be heard, and their proposals will be systemically implemented. But, there is no real demand for their opinion, either at the top level because of conservatism, or at the bottom level because of the lack of a social order.

Years slide by, the technocrats feel their uselessness, and they cease to believe first and foremost in themselves. They suffer from rational pessimism, the desire to be uninvolved, or to move to a different area of self-fulfillment. A negative signal for the society is the departure of these technocrats, which brings down the average level of competence in the economy, resulting in deceleration of economic transformation and stagnation. This creates conditions for paternalism to strengthen towards authoritarianism in response to crisis developments.

Authoritarianism and Dirigisme

Authoritarianism in the economy creates conditions for permissiveness, decision-making based on personal sympathies, and corruption. It creates uncertainty, avoidance of rules, and as Timothy Snyder put it in his book *The Road to Unfreedom,* it's the way to tyranny.[79] Therefore, common sense pushes businesses to adapt: agree in advance, 'lay the groundwork', get support from government bodies. Doing business without contact with executive and controlling government bodies becomes unnatural and evokes mutual discomfort. In the environment of authoritarianism, it is logical for businesses to provide assistance to the state by financing social, sports, public facilities, and events. While for businesses, these are expenses that can be attributed to transactional, corruption, costs in any case, for the state, it is a format of social equalisation, redistribution of excess profits, or a fee for the services of authoritarianism. The large number of restrictions and the amount of bureaucracy show that nothing can be done, but success stories prove that "it can be done somehow". American economist Robert Reich notes that, in such cases, the public looks up to their superiors, and believes that "if it is possible to do business on a large scale at the top, then it can be done on a small scale at the bottom".[80] It reduces the overall level of confidence in the economy. As a result, references to laws and regulations cause distrust, while personal recommendations generate respect.

In case of a cyclical 'thaw', paternalism takes the form of dirigisme. In the economy, this is reflected in attempts to guess what will be in demand, based on common sense and scientific evidence, identifying priority industries and projects, and directing state resources to those areas, specifically, to infrastructure, because of the stereotype of its durability, to agriculture and machine building because of inertia, or to other areas as a tribute to fashion. Investments in infrastructure (roads, airports) are believed to generate demand, although, on the contrary, they should be guided by demand. Investments in improving internet connectivity do not usually create a boom in e-commerce, unless there are other prerequisites for that, but rather just expand access to e-entertainment. In the face of the unlimited amount of conflicting information, dirigisme attempts to simplify the interpretation of economic developments in the process of decision-making. From time to time, decisions become spontaneous, generalising specific cases, or copying foreign experience. This leads to the emergence of original forms of the 'Cargo Cult',[81] when prototypes that have no real use are offered, just 'to have what others have'. The deeper dirigisme penetrates market relations, the more aware it becomes that it understands little, and it penetrates even further. As a result, expanding contacts with the unknown generates uncertainty in decision-making, which strengthens the orientation to short-term results and the past.

The main question for dirigisme in the economy is the following: Whose interests does it protect in decision-making? Is it some abstract society – the 'people'? Or are these specific people, many small groups that form the pluralism of different opinions and interests? Or are these businesses close to the dirigisme regime, the range of enterprises and industries, treated with personal sympathy and nostalgia?

In any case, decisions are made based on requests from one of the specified groups. And in the environment of paternalism, dirigisme normally protects the interests of businesses. Thus, 'because I decided so' may be the result of manipulation and non-public arrangements. In this way, dirigisme fosters businessmen relying on personal contacts, government support, and mining rent. At the same time, they should be distinguished from other businessmen, who have built their own businesses in a competitive environment, offering goods and services that have public utility and demand. Since decisions made in the context of dirigisme are driven by specific transactions and businesses, the entire economy is perceived as a series of mechanical manual processes.

Therefore, such abstract spheres as financial monetary relations are considered from the point of view of concrete interests and participants, to whom the responsibility is assigned. For instance, in the event of depreciation, these are speculators and bankers, who are made responsible, in the event of a budget deficit. These are those who do not pay taxes in the event of a drop in demand for products and incomes, these are enterprise managers, etc. There are historical records of such an approach to the economy. For example, back in 1124, startled by the pound sterling depreciation, and considering it to be a plot — although, in fact, the reason was the poor harvest and the subsequent jump in food prices — King Henry I gave orders to arrest about a hundred money men who were exchanging pounds, and amputate various parts of their body, up to castration.

The features of the Belarusian behavioural economics discussed above help decompose the premise 'because I decided so'. 'Because' characterises the often non-obvious and irrational nature of the business decisions offered by Belarusians. This is the answer to the silent question posed to them – "why?" 'I' is a sudden and uncontrollable manifestation of emotion and individualism, when 'my very myself' often overrides the collective 'we'. This is a consequence of internal permissiveness in the environment of the underdeveloped public and market checks and balances. 'Decided so' and 'only so' means that the main thing is that it should be done quickly, generating a visible, usually short-term result. And it should be clear, i.e. recognisable, as in the past, or as with others, as fashionable, at the very least. This is the effect of the orientation towards the Soviet past, short-term results, and paternalism in its different forms. 'Because I decided so' masks the choice by contradiction, avoiding disappointments, and preventing a negative scenario.

Poor economic decisions are backed by the self-justification and complacency of 'it could have been worse'. However, regrets about 'what could have been done' and 'what should have been done' are much weaker than the fear of 'making things worse than they are'. Financial incentives are dulled in decision-making, because the non-financial consequences of decisions (for instance, the war, the revolution) — sometimes contrived and projected by association from the past, or a similar situation — prevail. In general, decision-making in behavioural economics is based on the universal desire to simultaneously maintain the status quo, and control and implement the non-public (informal, shadow) arrangements. At the same time, the status quo is mobile and depends on changing expectations, which are also formed under the influence of the cultural matrix.

Summarising what has been said about the Belarusian cultural matrix and its impact on the economy, it should be noted that the latter is complex, both random and orderly.

The *randomness* is expressed in doublethink, swaying between collectivism and individualism, emotionality and restraint, the past and the future, short- and long-term, conservatism and liberalism. The unpredictable swings under the influence of doublethink resemble a 'drunken gait', when each subsequent step does not depend on the previous one, and is unknown even to the walker himself. In the theory of behaviourism, the first decision is usually considered irrational and incorrect (the so-called 'halo effect'),[82] while the second one is rational and more accurate.

In the case of Belarus, both decisions look irrational, and the Belarusian behavioural economics itself is akin to a set of anomalies. A decision can be affected by the unpredictable specific context, case, mood, fatigue, hunger, time of day, previous meeting, another person's statement, personality, association with the surname of the person in question, or something else that cannot be foreseen. All these are situational factors of the cultural matrix. Because of constant reflection and adaptation, the national features of psyche and local behavioural practices replace the classical economic theory and world practices, playing the priority and effective role in the Belarusian economy. Under the influence of the orientation towards short-term results, decisions are made at the last moment, quickly, under pressure, on the verge of guessing, and they are often considered, and turn out, to be correct. On the one hand, this gives the Belarusian economy a sense of stability and dynamism. On the other hand, it instils fragility and crisis thinking.

The *orderly* influence of the Belarusian matrix on the economy is reflected in the perceived influence of a range of cultural, economic, and other factors on the matrix itself and, thus, on the economy. Such factors are difficult to weigh and prioritise depending on their impact on the Belarusian economy. These are the 'tectonic plates' of the Belarusian behavioural economics, which overlap and move with time. They form the overall information and cultural environment, in which decisions are made, the values, which are shared by the public and combine into the cultural matrix, the unifying factors, which nowadays make the Belarusian matrix Belarusian, distinguishing it from other societies.

CHAPTER 4

BEHAVIOURAL ECONOMICS IN BELARUS

On 11 September 1941, Georgy Zhukov was appointed Commander of the Leningrad Front. He replaced Kliment Voroshilov, who had held that post for only a few days, since 5 September 1941, and had managed to distinguish himself by his inability to feel confident in the ever-changing situation, his stereotyped thinking, and avoiding responsibility after the humiliation of the Russo-Finnish War, running along trenches, revolver in hand, and personally leading attacks. In turn, Georgy Zhukov is best remembered for his painstaking, round-the-clock work with maps, operational and technical planning, resolving the most complicated problems of force supply and shifting amidst the Siege of Leningrad. At the same time, under Georgy Zhukov's command, there were retreat-blocking detachments, and executions for failure to comply with orders.

Analogies with the war emerge subconsciously when Belarusians face difficulties and seek solutions. It is important to pick the right cases from the information flow and learn the right lessons. The echo of the war is the background for Belarusian DNA; their collective memory, and is one of the deep-lying factors determining modern Belarusians and, oddly enough, affecting the economy.

Memories of the War

According to a sociological survey of 2013, 89.6% of Belarusians called the Great Patriotic War the main historical event for Belarusians.[83] To some extent, the collective memory of Belarusians about the Great Patriotic War forms their national identity, consolidating the society. That event, suffering, and victory have become sacred for Belarusians, and Independence Day (the day Minsk was liberated from Nazi invaders), holidays and memorial days, restored monuments, movies, names of central streets and squares, and awards timed to coincide with war memorial dates, underpin the national ideology.

When we return to Belarus after travelling in European countries, in the Czech Republic, France and Great Britain, we catch ourselves thinking how bare Belarus is. Everything was destroyed during the war and then rebuilt. Death camps were created in Belarus, and every Belarusian family suffered losses. The horrors of the war faced by Belarus are realistically shown in the Soviet drama of 1985, "Come and See". 'Never forget' is the credo of survivors, and is a constant reminder of the war, forming the orientation of the Belarusian society towards the Soviet past, orientation to scale, and association with the big victorious country.

Belarusians, however, remember the war not for its Victory Day, but mostly as a tragic event. About half of the respondents in Belarus (46.5%) perceive the May 9th holiday as "a day of remembrance and grief for all those who died", 28.5% as a "holiday of war veterans", and 20.9% as a "formal public holiday".[84] The collective memory of the tragedy of war shapes the focus on co-survival, i.e. collectivism, as well as the national identity, i.e., individualism. Armenians and Jews, for example, were able to unite and restore their statehood under the influence of the tragic memory of the genocide of their ancestors.

Cherishing memories of the war creates preconditions for militaristic thinking. The collapse of the USSR, the disorganisation of the former Soviet system in the absence of a vision for the future, and political sanctions, feed the military psychology of the Cold War and the occasional opposition between Belarus and the West, NATO, the EU, the US (even the IMF, and other international organizations). The militarisation of thinking influences the formation of features such as paternalism, as well as the more rigid form of authoritarianism.

The memories and fears of the war trigger the desire to seek protection from a strong leader. Military dirigisme leads to the construction of a system of economic management based on a military model, with the expectation that instructions will be followed like orders, and that if they are not, an associated liability, will be borne. Therefore, men in uniform, 'securocrats', and special secret services fit logically into the management system. On the one hand, the rigid structure of the management system and public life is formally supported, built according to rank and status, while on the other hand, there are cases where assignments do not conform with rank, or which jump several career steps or positions ahead, when a subordinate can suddenly become a boss. This leads to disorientation, weaker subordination, and discomfort in the vertical administrative structure.

The integration of military logic into the Belarusian economy makes it necessary to understand the war. What are the reasons for the victory, who are the heroes – state military leaders or ordinary soldiers? And, based on that, who should we bet on in the economy – ministers with subordinate enterprises, or businessmen? How should we perceive the price of victory, weighing the effects of military operations against human casualties? Drawing a parallel between the war and the economy, it is the price of the spent public wealth, the ratio of the budgetary support of an enterprise of any form of ownership to its contribution to GDP, to the tax revenues of the budget, to the job creation, and to the inflow of foreign exchange to the country.

Russian social scientists have formulated the main reason for victory in the Great Patriotic War as "...the personal initiative, which was generated owing to the ease of repression in the face of the common enemy. It was that initiative, which countervailed the paralysis and helplessness of the leadership. It was followed by the emergence of a sense of personal responsibility for the fate of the country and the development of the skills of freedom". In the context of the war, the public was seen by the authorities as a temporary ally rather than as an object of repression and control.[85] As an illustration, it should be mentioned that during that hard period there was even a slight return to religion, with many churches reopened and clergymen engaged in praying during military operations.

It is also important to note that during the war there was also a different system of decision-making. In his memoirs, Anastas Mikoyan, Deputy Chairman of the Council of People's Commissars, Council of Ministers of the USSR, wrote: "Stalin did not call any official meetings. Issues were usually resolved promptly, as they arose, by a narrow group of Politburo members. Having realised that at that difficult time the Politburo was to work in a healthy way, Stalin created an atmosphere of trust, and each of us, members of the Politburo, carried a huge load. We worked successfully owing to the underlying trust. We often resolved major problems by making telephone calls or giving an instruction in a meeting. We resorted to issuing written documents very rarely. And I must say, that in the first three years of the war there was a great atmosphere for the friendly work of all of us. It was only in the last year [of the war], when the victory was evident, and the country was almost liberated, that Stalin, not without some help from Beria, but rather on his initiative, reintroduced paperwork in our operation".[86]

The conclusion that victory was secured largely thanks to the people, their instinct of self-preservation, and the atmosphere of trust created in the administrative apparatus, contradicts the established ideology of the USSR that victory was won "thanks to the might of the Soviet state". This ideological collision, also inherited by Belarus, does not allow

Belarusians to employ military logic beneficially to exit from the economic crisis.

Instead of granting entrepreneurial freedom for self-survival, Belarus preserves the inert military mentality of the strong role of the state and paternalism. This leads to increased control over businesses, maintaining the traditionally high budgetary expenditures on poorly performing enterprises, accompanied by the decreasing incomes of the population.

Instead of establishing a trusting environment for the development and consistent implementation of a long-term strategy to exit the crisis, there is continued orientation towards short-term results and personal involvement in solving immediate tasks. This impedes the development of a vision of a way out of the crisis.

The military mentality in the modern Belarusian crisis economy underlies the different values and dimensions of power and society, which form the doublethink and the patchy collective identity.

Family-Orientation

Another cultural factor that determines the Belarusian matrix is family-orientation. It forms the dualism of collectivism and individualism. It unites and separates at the same time. It narrows the circle of trust, range of partners, limits behavioural practices, and restrains social identity. In addition, such features as paternalism and orientation towards the Soviet past are formed under the influence of Belarusian family-orientation. The stereotypes that determine the matrix and influence the economy are formed within the family, at the husband-wife, 'parents-children' levels. Among the many stereotypes of the Belarusian family, we can highlight the following:

First: Women should keep house and raise children. This stereotype is a feature of orientation to the past. According to the results of a survey into the use of time, women in Belarus tend to spend twice as much time on housekeeping and raising children as men, and have 20% less spare time.[87] In general, a large proportion of Belarusians (43%) believe that "the wife must always obey her husband".[88] This is a prerequisite for economic violence within the family, and discrimination in financial behaviour. For example, men in developing countries are reported to spend money primarily on cigarettes, alcohol, and their own entertainment, while women tend to spend money on their households and children, rather than on their own needs. Economic rights are usually distributed unevenly – men control cash and property, while women are entrusted with household duties and responsibilities. At the same time, since they spend money more frugally, females are more attractive borrowers than men. Men tend to help in caring for children depending on their mood, and not on the need for help. This is also related to the desire to avoid conflict with the child's mother. Such domestic behaviour reduces men's credibility among women. In addition, in the context of orientation to the past in raising children, men tend to motivate by threats. In the past, respect for one's father was instilled through fear, when every appearance of the father-breadwinner in the family was seen as an exam. Today, respect for one's father is nurtured through mutual understanding and mutual interests, which entails joint pastimes and more frequent communication.

One of the reasons for this stereotype in Belarus is that there are fewer men than women and, should divorce occur, men have a wider choice and better chances of finding a new partner. This serves as a prerequisite for the high level of divorce in the country, with over 400 divorces per 1,000 marriages in Belarus. Therefore, men are less likely to socialise with their families, often live 'in a world of their own', are sometimes unpredictable, less responsible, more aggressive, more likely to abuse alcohol, and are prone to violence. Eliminating the stereotype of the 'medieval man' is possible if couples see their relationships as long-term. Then they become more equal and support each other. In addition, men can be encouraged to maintain permanent and long-term family relationships if divorce is made unprofitable for them. In other countries, this is ensured through large alimony payments or lifetime support of the first wife.

Second: Men should pursue their careers and earn more. This stereotype creates conditions for the development of paternalism. In the Belarusian family, men (71.4% of responses) are more oriented toward professional self-realisation than women (61%), and for women, the family can become a barrier to employment (43.4%), promotion (28.7%), and training (27.7%).[89] However, this stereotype is primarily a trap for men in the absence of a guaranteed lifelong career. Loss of work is regarded by men as a tragedy, as demoralising, and leads to depression and the avoidance of reality through alcohol abuse (which is the main cause of divorce in Belarus), social networks, and gambling. At the same time, a man who has lost his job does not always switch to housekeeping, he usually does nothing, waiting for better times.

It would be beneficial to all to dismantle this stereotype. For a man, it would provide the opportunity to devote more time to his family and children and to avoid stress at work, which affects his health and longevity. For a woman, it would provide extra time for her career, hobby, home, and family. For children, such a family would then become the model projected to future generations. It is possible to remove these cultural barriers by overcoming the constraints associated with women's access to the labour market and promotion, through levelling the retirement age and reducing the length of parental leave. According to some estimates, if parental leave is shortened from 2017, the growth rate of the Belarusian economy could increase by 2.3% annually, with the long-term positive effect declining, while a gradual levelling of the retirement age could generate additional real GDP growth of more than 1% each year from 2019, further increasing the positive effect for the economy. Taken together, the two gender factors could lead to an increase in Belarus' real GDP by 2.7% in 2017, 3.1% in 2018, 3.4% in 2019, 3.7% in 2020, and by almost 13% in 2021, compared to 2016.[90] Similar estimates are offered in a study of the consequences of closing the gender gap in developing countries in 2015-2020. The GDP growth could be from 9% in Brazil to 27% in India, and 34% in Egypt.[91]

Third: Sharing a home with their children negatively affects parents' relationships. This stereotype fosters doublethink, suggesting a mental gap between generations. On the one hand, it pushes towards pronounced individualism, and the desire of children to escape from the cultural matrix, to avoid paternalism and collectivism. On the other hand, it causes paternalism, since, in practice, parents share their home with their children not because it is a desirable situation, but largely because their children are unable to be financially autonomous at the initial stage of their independence. In addition, paternalism takes various forms, since different generations interpret who should provide financial support to whom in different ways. In this regard, in the case of home sharing, there are prerequisites for economic discrimination and orientation toward saving to purchase real estate.

However, this is only a stereotype and is not always confirmed empirically. According to the results of the survey of Belarusians, conducted by the Institute of Sociology of the National Academy of Sciences of Belarus in 2013-2014, the fact of whether or not children and parents share a home has no impact on their relationships. Constant communication is a preferable basis of relationships between parents and children. The need to provide financial support to parents was ranked somewhat lower. The statement that "parents should help their children financially through all their lives" received a comparable ranking. In the opinion of Belarusians, providing support should be a two-way process between the two generations – parents and children.

Language

Language is sometimes considered the basic factor of any cultural matrix. According to the principle of linguistic relativity, or the Sapir–Whorf hypothesis, language differences determine differences in culture, psyche, and behaviour. As an illustration, differences in language, the logic of building words and sentences, can explain some of the mental differences between Japanese and Germans, and Chinese and Russians. Japanese and Chinese are reflective, they think in abstract terms, images and hieroglyphics. Germans are straightforward, with orderly sentences and speech. Owing to their language, which allows a differentiation of shades, Russians are multi-active and emotional. Israeli linguist Guy Deutscher distinguishes shades of light blue (*goluboi*) and dark blue (*sinij*), which exist in Russian, but are not found in English (blue), and which influence the differences in the outlooks of the two cultures.[92] American researcher Malcolm Gladwell explains China's economic success by the excellence of Chinese schoolchildren in mathematics, which is, among other things, attributed to the ease of pronouncing figures in the Chinese language: *yī* (one), *èr* (two), *sān* (three), *sì* (four), *wǔ* (five), etc.[93]

However, there are theories and examples that disprove the link between language, culture, and economics. According to the theory of American linguist Noam Chomsky, the grammar principles underlying a language are inborn, therefore differences in languages can be explained by the parametric settings of the brain, and not by differences in cultures. There are examples, when people speaking the same language have substantial differences in their mentality and standards of living. For instance, French is used both in France and in the countries of the former French colonies in Africa. Portuguese is spoken in Portugal and Brazil. English is used in the UK and Nigeria.

Or there are examples where people speaking different languages form common values, have similarities in their mentality and demonstrate a certain amount of synchrony in their economic development. In this case, multilingualism is not an obstacle to the formation of regional cultural matrices, specifically the European matrix in EU countries, the Soviet matrix in the USSR, or the Asian matrix in the ASEAN countries.

Bilingualism is of practical interest in the context of Belarus. On the one hand, it can be regarded as an advantage, as it allows the building of the logic of thinking, talking, and behaviour, in different ways, and to look for compromise. Bilingualism can offer additional opportunities if we are talking about widely used languages such as English, Chinese, and Spanish. On the other hand, bilingualism can lead to doublethink if it involves a merger of the corresponding cultures. However, language is separated from culture in the modern world, becoming rather a tool of communication, while culture acquires an interethnic status. For example, the use of English and French in Canada, Chinese and Malay in Singapore, and German and French in Switzerland.

I must admit that bilingualism in Belarus is not fully-fledged. Russian is the main spoken language, it is the language used for writing documents, and the language of thought, while the Belarusian language is actually foreign for many. Russian, in Belarus, is not just the language of communication. It largely determines many Belarusian features, for example, the orientation towards the Soviet past, hence the orientation to scale, to short-term planning and paternalism, as well as individualism in the form of isolation from the rest of the world. In this regard, learning a foreign language becomes an incentive for getting out of the existing cultural matrix, and provides an opportunity for competitive employment in other countries.

In the framework of the Belarusian management system, the use of the Russian language leads to limited communication, the adoption of the international experience through Russia, and relevant joint orientation for the future. Foreign language skills and knowledge of multicultural norms and values become a rare advantage, rather than a natural quality, in the management system of Belarus. In this regard, the so-called 'Western' elite — which may include managers of any developed country, whether Western or Eastern — are not able to find a common language with the Belarusian elite, and, moreover, feel increasingly uncomfortable about such contacts. In turn, the Belarusian side perceives this as arrogance and disrespect, which further alienates Western and Belarusian managers. At the same time, the use of the Russian language naturally leads to the mental rapprochement of the national elites of Belarus and Russia. It is also reinforced by a certain orientation of the Belarusian society to the Russian cultural matrix, which is conditioned, for instance, by the remaining friend and kinship ties. According to a sociological survey conducted in 2016, 38.4% of Belarusians reported that they have friends and relatives in Russia.[94]

The use of the Russian language in the Belarusian economy predetermines the orientation of its foreign trade, investments, and tourism to Russian-speaking partners. The predominant use of the Russian language for official purposes in government bodies, by businesses, to make street signs, in taxis and public transport, in Belarus, creates a natural barrier and increases the costs for non-Russian-speaking trading partners, investors, and tourists. In addition, there is social pressure from the public to oust foreign languages from communication. This creates a competitive advantage for businesses and tourists from Russian-speaking countries.

In general, it is important to emphasise that the author's intention is not to drive the reader to cultural decoding or to criticism of the Russian language and its replacement by another language, including Belarusian. The point is that the exclusive orientation of the economy to the Russian language results in a failure to take advantage of other, more competitive and promising, languages (for example, English and Chinese). Their inadequate use in the Belarusian economy results in an unjustified loss of business opportunities.

Sense of Ownership

On returning to Belarus from a summer vacation abroad, many friends share their impressions, speaking not so much about the sea, the sun, and interesting people, but of how tasty the food was. When I raised the question of why food in Belarusian restaurants is not always considered delicious, and started to interview restaurant-keepers, I was told "it's delicious when the food is cooked by the restaurant owner". This explains the popularity of small cafes in Europe, diners in China, and eateries in the Middle East. Small private businesses offer not only cheap, but also delicious, food, and this price-quality ratio improves the overall competitiveness of the society.

Another example of how a sense of ownership affects human behaviour was presented by financial journalist Rachel Botsman. She explained that a person staying at a hotel leaves towels on the bathroom floor, while someone staying at an Airbnb accommodation always carefully hangs the towels up, out of respect to the property of the house owner.[95] This behaviour forms mutual trust between strangers, and within the society as a whole.

This sense of ownership forms healthy individualism, generating the collective energy necessary for economic progress. It is this sense, manifested from early childhood, that grows into the sense of belonging to society and the state, and the sense of ownership of one's territory, land, and country. This is achieved through the sense of 'mine, not mine', responsibility for decisions, involvement, and empathy. In Belarus, the collective memory, orientation towards the Soviet past, orientation to scale, and paternalism, all dull the sense of ownership. This affects the public's attitude to large, state-owned, enterprises as features of heritage and culture, which then constrains their privatisation and restructuring.

Doublethink also affects the sense of ownership in Belarus, as its cultivated sense of community and state ownership are combined with the skills of private ownership acquired by the youngest generation of Belarusians. The transition from one sense to another, from state ownership to private, and back, is perceived by the public in a very specific way. Under the influence of the management system and the information background, privatisation in Belarus and private investors' participation in the capital of state-owned enterprises are seen as "shedding something unnecessary, inefficient and unhealthy". In other words, if a state-owned enterprise is successful, there is no sense in changing the owner. In turn, nationalisation is reflected in the public mind as a way of saving a company, which is specifically perceived as 'dying' because, following its privatisation, it changed its business profile, was restructured, and adapted to economic reality.

Doublethink, in the sense of ownership, programmes the failure of state-owned enterprise modernisation. On the one hand, it creates an opportunity for abuse, corruption, and theft - for example, when equipment procurement is financed from the budget. In addition, this abuse is unconsciously perceived as a kind of fair transition of part of state-owned property to private ownership, or as a natural fee for management services. On the other hand, the modernisation is accompanied by negligence, red tape, and hack-work, treating project implementation as a temporary task, which is supported by an understanding of why tenants do not renovate rented apartments.

Fear

Going back to the story presented at the beginning of this chapter about the appointment of Georgy Zhukov as Commander of the Leningrad Front, many readers could have focused on the facts specifically mentioned in passing – executions for failure to comply with orders and retreat-blocking detachments positioned to shoot their own troops in the event of their retreat. Many could conclude that it was fear, rather than Zhukov's strategic planning and adaptation to the changing environment, that produced his military victories. Fear is the key motivating factor of the Soviet man, and the projector of the Soviet past onto the Belarusian society. It would be wrong to say that fear is inherent only in the Soviet man. Under the influence of historical events, it is deeply rooted in any matrix. And it is sometimes so deeply engrained that it self-reflects, and the matrix becomes the source of fear, affecting the economic behaviour of people.

There are plenty of historical examples of negative economic developments experienced by society which affect the economic behaviour and economic policies of future generations.

As an illustration, in 1980, US inflation reached 13.8%, which was unusual and frightening. In this regard, in order to bring inflation down by attracting foreign capital and strengthening the US dollar, Paul Volcker, Chairman of the Board of Governors of the Federal Reserve System, raised the interest rate to 19% in 1981. By 1986, inflation had fallen to 1.9% and then, for decades, became the main indicator of economic policy to dispel the inflationary fears and expectations of the population dating back to those years.[96]

Another example is Germany. Because of the collective memory of the hyperinflation of the 1920s, and the Great Depression, the denial of consumer loans is deeply rooted in the 'German character'. Therefore, German politicians know they would not be supported if they built their pre-election programmes around borrowing and risks of financial instability. It was largely due to this phobia that Germany managed to avoid the consequences of the global financial crisis of 2008.[97]

In Belarus, phobias explain many of the features of its behavioural economics. The fear of losing earnings, perhaps because of their depreciation due to inflation, exceeds the willingness to earn more, which creates a greater propensity to save than to invest. The fear of losing a job with a change of owner, following the example of Russia in the 1990s, creates a cautious attitude towards privatisation. The fear of the future, and disappointment in the present, form the orientation to the past in the search for answers. The fear of punishment, both inherited and learned, serves as a habitual motivation in the paternalistic regime. It holds back, delays decision-making, and leads to a situation where the person responsible for the issue 'vanishes', stops responding to phone calls and messages, and 'avoids' meetings. The fear of 'wiretapping' sometimes results in commercial negotiations with state-owned enterprises being conducted in whispers in the corridor, or outside, to avoid random words being misinterpreted and misreported. The risk and fear of making a mistake in the state apparatus is not compensated by anything. As a result, rational behaviour and the bureaucratic norm is "not to deviate from regulations and the course", "to follow clear, written instructions" or "do nothing".

The orientation towards the Soviet past makes it habitual and rational in a certain sense to use prisoners in the Belarusian economy, to give an opportunity to officially 'buy off' justice. The practice of the General Directorate of Camps (GULAG), established under the NKVD in 1930 by the State Planning Committee of the USSR to speed up the implementation of the first Soviet Five-Year Plan, is increasingly referred to as an analogy when it is necessary to discipline and motivate the Belarusian economy. It is interesting to note that the system of Soviet five-year plans of economic development, inherited by Belarus, was correlated to the five-year terms of imprisonment in Soviet times, which facilitated the planning of labour resources for industrialisation.

The orientation towards the Soviet past hinders the development of Belarusian entrepreneurship. If the older generation experienced a collective fear of the state and restrictions of their economic freedom, they would hardly recommend their children to defend their rights and take business risks. The older generation is faced with the contradiction of "we suffered, and our children are doomed to suffer" and "we suffered, but our children should not suffer". In any case, the result is the collective type of behaviour characterised by a low level of entrepreneurial risk.

At present, the atmosphere of fear in the Belarusian economy is formed by the information background. The rhetoric in the management system, based on mentioning punishment, criminal liability, regular reports on detentions, court proceedings against officials responsible for the economy, heads of state-owned enterprises, and owners of private businesses, raises anxiety. It can be noted that, in recent years, key economic news and reports in Belarus come from the courtroom rather than the stock exchange. This affects the moods and behaviour of economic agents, and forms the behaviour of a person who, moving forward, constantly looks back and around, which slows his progress.

In general, the fear of making a mistake, breaking the law, losing one's savings, job, and health, is a sufficiently pronounced factor of the Belarusian matrix, affecting the economy. According to the sociological survey of Belarusians' phobias conducted in December 2016, 50.2% of respondents mentioned a rise in prices for food and essential goods, 39.1% – a drop in salaries and wages, 38.3% – utility tariff hikes, 34.3% –

inflation and currency depreciation, and 32.3% – the health condition. Thus, the main fears of Belarusians are hidden in the economic code, or more precisely in the monetary sphere.

Memory of Depreciations

Over the past 25 years, Belarus has become a record holder for currency crises among the countries of the former USSR – its depreciations are longer, more frequent, and deeper. In terms of 1991 roubles, by January 2016, the US dollar exchange rate to the currencies of the countries that, together with Belarus, originate from the Soviet Union, would have been the following: Latvia – 1 to 130, Estonia – 1 to 144, Lithuania – 1 to 319, Russia – 1 to 79,993, Kazakhstan – 1 to 193,657, Ukraine – 1 to 2,470,000, and Belarus – 1 to 215,640,000.[98] Accordingly, it has affected inflation, which is almost always at the two-digit level. Over the history of its independent monetary policy, Belarus has had single-digit inflation three times: in 2005 (7.9%), in 2006 (6.6%), and in 2010 (9.9%). In all other years, it had two-digit and three-digit inflation. The memory of depreciation in Belarus includes several dramatic periods and episodes:

1) 1992-1996: collapse of the USSR, introduction of own local currency, hyperinflation. During that period, the Belarusian rouble depreciated vis-à-vis the US dollar by a factor of 900(!);
2) 1996-2000: multiple exchange rates, at a certain point in time there were up to eight parallel exchange rates. During that period, the US dollar exchange rate grew by a factor of over 100(!) from BYR 11,500 to BYR 1,180,000;
3) 2 January 2009: during one day, the exchange rate vis-à-vis the US dollar depreciated by 20%, from BYR 2,200 to BYR 2,650, with the redenomination factored in;
4) 24 May 2011: the exchange rate depreciated in one step by over 50% from BYR 3,155 to BYR 4,930 per US dollar, and by 21 October 2011, it had depreciated further, by 75%, reaching BYR 8,680 per US dollar;
5) 2012-2014: depreciation reached no more than BYR 10 per day, and made slightly over 30% for three years. By 19 December 2014, the exchange rate was BYR 11,500;

6) 2015 – today. In 2015, depreciation was 29.4%. By mid-2017, the exchange rate to the US dollar reached about BYR 18,700, with the redenomination not factored in.

Here is the key question: Why is this happening? The world history of currency crises offers a few textbook examples.

In the 18th century, Scottish financier John Law put forth his theory that it is possible to create money, finance large projects, improve the wellbeing of the people and, at the same time, have no consumer price growth. In France, John Law eased into the confidence of the Duke of Orleans, who helped him create a money emission bank in 1716, and granted a few monopolies, including that of the tobacco trade, as well as France's foreign trade with Louisiana, Africa, and eventually with all countries outside Europe.

The substance of John Law's theory was to issue his company shares and simultaneously issue banknotes to buy these shares, which contributed to their price growth. At the same time, the money received by Law's company was spent on the implementation of major projects (in the end, none was successful). In 1720, influenced by the rumours and forecasts of sceptics, the shareholders of the company began to exchange their shares for gold and silver. In response, John Law introduced restrictions on the exchange and, most importantly, stopped the emission, which dumped the stock price. When the emission was renewed, the stock price was fixed, supported with interventions. At the same time, the amount of money in circulation was growing, inflation increased, and the population continued to exchange company shares for metallic money, depleting the reserves of France. Under this pressure, John Law relinquished the stock price and had to flee France.

In Belarus, the reasons for the incessant depreciations are rooted in national features such as paternalism, orientation to the past, orientation to scale, and orientation to short-term results. Due to the desire to quickly finance large-scale projects that solve social problems, such as providing housing and food, emission money was directed to the construction sector and agriculture. It boosted both economic growth and inflation. Support through money emission was also granted to industrial enterprises and banks, which did not generate comparable foreign exchange returns. Given the lack of foreign exchange reserves, the money emission was unsecured, while the low level of confidence and poor development of other financial instruments resulted in a feverish demand for foreign exchange, which consistently undermined the exchange rate and led to a new upsurge in inflation. The memory of incessant depreciations formed the propensity of the population to save by keeping foreign currency cash 'under the mattress'. That modelled a specific type of fast high-yield and, therefore, high-risk, and at times, shadow business, the pace of which outstripped that of depreciation. But, most importantly, the distrust in the national currency and monetary authorities has become deeply rooted in Belarusians over the years.

Loss of confidence in monetary authorities is rarely recovered. It is noteworthy that any public appearance of the heads of monetary authorities associated with devaluations — no matter what they say, or whether they say anything at all — results in a surge of the depreciation expectations of the population. For example, in 2013, 'reassuring' speeches by a number of senior officials were followed by one-day surges in currency purchases, which exceeded those made on normal days by USD 15-20 million. Since 2015, the attitude of the public towards monetary authorities has become more neutral, despite the continued instability of the exchange rate. This can be explained by the fact that the National Bank has stopped the practice of undertaking obligations to maintain a fixed exchange rate and switched to a floating market exchange rate. At the same time, *the exchange rate can hardly be a market one in a non-market economy*. It creates doublethink. Thus, it is not only monetary, but all economic authorities that are responsible for currency stability. But the *de facto* responsibility for currency stability is shifted to external markets (oil, potassium, Russia) and ultimately to the population and businesses. In the monetary sphere, the population relies mainly on senior officials in view of both paternalism and the ultimate authority they have in clearing and mobilising loans to maintain currency stability.

The confidence in economic authorities could be restored only on condition that government intervention in both the monetary sphere and the overall economy is limited. However, it contradicts such Belarusian features as paternalism, which implies control over financial resources, which predetermines incessant depreciations. The solution is to stop relying on the services of the central bank as the regulator of the monetary sphere, shifting this function to the so-called currency board, which would link the size of foreign exchange reserves with the money supply, establish a fixed exchange rate and, thereby, ensure the currency stability needed to implement other economic policies. An unexpected future alternative to this may be the voluntary abandonment of the unstable and constantly depreciating national currency by Belarusians and their transition to a crypto currency. Forecasts have been made for the use of cryptocurrency as an alternative to unsustainable local currencies, for example in Argentina, Venezuela and Iraq.[99]

Memory of Loss of Savings

The collapse of the Soviet Union left a deep imprint in the collective memory, not so much because of the ideological loss — there was no faith left in communism by that time — but because of the instantaneous massive loss of savings and impoverishment of the people. The 'perished' Soviet deposits, vouchers, inflation, depreciation, and the banking crisis of the 1990s, translated into the tragedy of human lives, a generation gap, a change of values, and cultural shock. The loss of savings is deeply engrained in people's memory, as it was instantaneous and irreversible. It is for this reason that the Belarusian society took one-off depreciations and price jumps much harder than gradual changes in the exchange rate and moderate inflation. In general, losing everything at once is the greatest fear one could experience, and the consequences of that are the most painful and memorable. Humans adapt to small evolutionary changes naturally, more quickly and easily, and sometimes even do not fully realise them. It's like entering the water gradually or adding boiling water little by little, when one is already submerged. This psychological attribute, which is associated with missing out on small changes, enables the implementation of unpopular economic policy measures, which are 'inconspicuous' for the public – a gradual increase in taxes, prices, smooth currency depreciation, etc.

The sudden humiliating poverty of the post-Soviet period, shutting the door on people's faith and life goals, will linger long in the memory of Belarusians. At the same time, the public tends to confuse cause and effect. The liberal, market-oriented policies, which inherited and solved economic problems, rather than the conservative policies, which created those problems, are sometimes called the root cause of the difficulties. The unlearned lessons of the causes of the economic crisis of the Soviet Union, the change of generations, the period of over 25 years that has passed since then, dull the memory of the loss of savings. This weakens financial discipline and creates prerequisites for another financial and economic crisis. In this regard, the memory of the loss of savings can be treated as a skinned, but not healing wound, which may reopen and affect the future of the economy if a crisis similar to the Soviet one occurs. At present, the prerequisites for this are found in the unsustainable financial pyramid built in recent years with government and quasi-government debt.

Debt pyramids appear when old debts are converted into new ones. As American economist Irving Fisher put it at the time of the Great Depression, "the more debtors pay, the more they owe". The same happens in Belarus. Belarus' external government debt is not repaid with proceeds from its use, and is partially refinanced, being shifted to the future. Non project-related government loans are used to replenish reserves, and to refinance old debts, and do not generate foreign exchange proceeds through exports and foreign direct investments. Due to problems with business plan appraisal and monitoring, project-related external government loans and guarantees do not always generate foreign exchange proceeds either, and are sometimes repaid by the budget rather than by the projects. In turn, external debt refinancing with the more expensive domestic debt leads to an increase in the size of the aggregate government debt and an outflow of foreign exchange from the country, due to the weakening of the banks' resource base and the declining foreign exchange savings of households.

Debt pyramids are unsustainable when the debt rule is broken – "government loans should stimulate economic growth, and the rate of economic growth should exceed that of government debt". This has recently become a new abnormal norm for many countries. Until 2007, the GDP growth of USD 1 had been accompanied by an increase in debt by USD 1 in most developing countries, in 2012 this ratio went up to 1 to 2, and in a number of countries, such as China, it reached 1 to 3.[100] In 2015-2016, the increase in the government debt in Belarus was accompanied by a fall in its GDP. As a result, the ratio of government debt to GDP increased in Belarus from 22.3% as of 1 January 2015, to 39.4% as of 1 January 2017. But, in view of the fact that Belarusian government debt is mainly denominated in foreign currency, the key indicators for payments related thereto include net exports, foreign direct investment, and the ability to attract new loans. When the first two parameters decrease, the main focus becomes new loans.

Debt pyramids collapse when the inflow of new loans stops. It is symbolic that in economic theory this point is called the 'Minsky Moment', after American economist Hyman Minsky, the son of Belarusian emigrants, who took his surname in honour of the city of Minsk upon their arrival in the US. According to his theory, which regained its popularity after the 2008 US mortgage crisis, there are three types of borrowers. Those belonging to the first type hedge their risks, manage flows, and can avoid default. Those of the second type are only able to pay interest on loans but cannot repay the principal amount. The third type cannot rely on their cash flows, but only on the growing value of their assets. The 'Minsky Moment' comes when the asset value stops growing.

Belarus as a borrower can be superficially classified under the first type. But it has a specific feature, and if this is factored in, Belarus moves closer to the second type of borrower. Faced with a limited range of external creditors in recent years, Belarus *de facto* focused on borrowing from a single creditor. The new external loans mobilised from Russian banks, the EurAsEC Fund, and the Government of Russia, are actually controlled by one creditor. This narrows the space for manoeuvre in government debt management and creates new risks. The worst thing in cases of problems with several creditors is a default and the loss of access to the international financial market for three to four years; with one creditor it is a matter of sovereignty.

Until 2012, Belarus attracted resources from international markets, although these transactions were often predetermined, that is, Belarusian and Russian banks often bought sovereign bonds. After 2012, almost all non-project-related government loans were extended for political reasons. At the same time, government debt management instruments, such as syndicated loans, issuance of municipal, corporate bonds in foreign markets, and so on, were practically never used. In 2017, Belarus once again tapped the international financial market, issuing its Eurobonds worth USD 1.4 billion to refinance old debts and somewhat diversify the pool of its external creditors.

How are the government debt problems related to the loss of household savings? Warren Buffett, a well-known American financier, wrote: "you only find out who is swimming naked when the tide goes out". If the inflow of external loans stops, the natural reaction of regulators would be a 'reboot' – a recapitalisation of the financial and credit system *inter alia* using the existing foreign exchange deposits of households.

Until 2020, the annual payments in foreign exchange associated with the government debt will exceed USD 2 billion. At the same time, the liquid foreign exchange reserves of the National Bank are also over USD 2 billion. With bank and government guarantees and resources entwined, and the share of bad assets growing — from 4.4% as of 1 January 2015 to 12.8% as of 1 January 2017 — the banking system cannot be a reliable source of foreign exchange debt refinancing.

In the context of a further deterioration of exports, combined with an outflow of foreign direct investments and a sudden cessation of new foreign loan inflows, a sharp devaluation will call for the suspension of banking operations, exchanges, the money market, and a 'freezing' of deposits due to an inability to fulfil all government obligations to creditors, including foreign and domestic banks. In their turn, banks, which consider government bonds to be the most reliable kind of assets and have built their own pyramids based on that, will be forced to renege on their obligations, including those to households.

Addressing the accumulated challenges without destroying the debt pyramid would call for a change in economic policies and a voluntary moratorium on mobilising new government guaranteed loans. It would also involve opening the economy up for non-debt sources of financing, i.e. foreign direct investment. However, a voluntary declaration of a moratorium and, most importantly, its disciplined implementation, are unlikely. It takes self-control to change. But it usually appears under the pressure of a default.

Following this logic, the earlier the debt pyramid is destroyed, the fewer people will be affected. If the pyramid is too big, when it collapses, everybody will be affected. A massive loss of savings would reopen old social wounds, which can influence the future decisions of authorities, for example, opting not to borrow new loans for a long time. In the long run it would have a beneficial effect, but in the short term, it would weaken the ability of the economy to quickly build its growth trend, even with its transition to generally rational economic policies.

Instinct of Survival

The collective memory of the war, loss of savings, depreciations, fear, and locking in family-orientation, all hone Belarusians' survival instinct. In one form or another, this factor affects the matrix of many peoples. The more difficulties the population faces (for example, war, terrorism, poverty), the more the survival instinct manifests itself. In the matrix of Belarusians, it is reflected in individualism – "every man for himself". When difficulties turn systemic and universal, Belarusians display self-organising collectivism.

In the economy, this factor is manifested through self-employment. As unemployment grows and real incomes fall, the logical behaviour is to switch from employment in state-owned enterprises to that in the private sector and self-employment. As an illustration, in 2011, the state-owned sector employed 44% of all labour resources and the private sector accounted for 56%, while in 2016, the respective shares were 40% and 60%.

The self-employed, i.e. those simultaneously functioning as the employee and the employer, can include border traders, shuttle traders, unregistered construction workers, farmers, tutors, private taxi drivers, family members working without registration, students, pensioners, and others. It is difficult to determine their exact number. It would be correct to consider not only official, but also 'hidden unemployment', i.e. accounting for forced unpaid or partially paid leave, a partial working week, hours rather than days worked, etc. But in any case, there are self-employed people in Belarus, and their number is growing.

According to the Economy Research Institute of the Ministry of Economy, in 2012, there were 182,700 self-employed people, which accounted for 3% of the labour force. Over recent years, the number of self-employed people has grown because of the cuts in high-paying jobs, efforts to lower the labour costs at state-owned enterprises, optimisation of the state apparatus, and unwillingness to retire due to a sharp drop in social status and income levels. According to various estimates, by early 2017, there were more than 420,000 self-employed people, which accounted for about 10% of the labour force. Thus, year by year, 'shadow' employment becomes the new norm, the 'rational' economic thinking, which is a step towards the formation of individual entrepreneurialism. Therefore, relatively few people in Belarusian society are concerned about the risk of unemployment. According to the sociological survey of December 2016, only 15.2% of Belarusians are concerned about the risk of losing their jobs – most of all in Gomel region (23.2%) and least of all in Mogilev region (9.7%). In response to the direct question "Do you personally face the risk of losing your job?", 5.9% of respondents answered "yes", 10.8% chose the option "most likely yes", while others did not consider this a risk.

In the Belarusian economy, the instinct to survive (individualism) becomes stronger in the context of an economic crisis and is dulled by paternalism and an orientation to the Soviet past. In Belarus, as well as in the Soviet Union, the unemployed are perceived as 'parasites', and as a socially unstable and active element able to invoke social instability. In this regard, there is doublethink in treating them. On the one hand, they do receive some support, and employment centres are created. On the other hand, repressive measures such as fines, penalties, criminal liability, etc., are applied.

However, administrative measures mainly reveal some shadow businesses avoiding taxes, as well as partially informal and illegal relations in industries with a high turnover, and high salaries (in manufacturing, trade, construction, banking). The number of violations detected is constantly growing, but it is rather an indicator that the shadow economy is growing, while repressive measures, taken alone, are unable to restrain it effectively.

Therefore, it is expedient to take economic measures to improve the competitiveness of 'shadow businesses' and 'bring them out to the light' by streamlining taxes, offering cheaper loans, and ensuring further red tape reduction. At the same time, the effectiveness of economic measures (for example, capital legalisation) largely depends on the credibility of the state. Among other things, shadow businesses are reluctant to come out into the light, because of their fear of new repressive measures that may follow the legalisation of their incomes.

The contradiction between the instinct for survival and paternalism could be resolved by building mutual trust between the employed (not only self-employed) and the state, developing the necessary infrastructure – centres for retraining and job search, a system of private pension funds, etc.

On the part of the employed, it would involve the creation of fully-fledged trade unions acting as intermediaries, protecting the interests of workers against employers and the state, and lobbying for benefits in new enterprises, or progressive income tax rates. The aim of trade unions should be to ensure the equal rights of employees and shareholders of enterprises, since the latter are not the only ones investing and adding value to the enterprise. A successful example of such a business model can be found in China, in Huawei, a company where the employees are simultaneously the shareholders.

On the part of the state, this would entail the creation of jobs, though not only new wage-paying jobs, but jobs that are interesting and have good career prospects, and are therefore more attractive to people. Here it is reasonable to bring in the example of a visit of Milton Friedman, a Nobel Memorial Prize laureate in Economic Sciences, to a construction site in the 1960s. He saw that workers were digging with shovels and asked why there were no excavators. The answer was that that was how jobs were created. In response, the economist sarcastically offered to replace shovels with spoons, which would create even more jobs.[101]

In conclusion, it is important to remember that the cultural matrix itself only influences the economy, it does not define it. It should not cause unreasonable self-confidence, self-deception, abandonment of economic reality, or substitution of economic laws and mechanisms.

Thus, returning to the analogies with the Second World War, we can recall the memoirs of one of the military commanders of that time. He described how at the time, when the enemy was approaching the capital and the associated economic difficulties were mounting, some hope suddenly arose that one could achieve success even with primitive weapons. There was growing confidence that the technical inefficiency of weapons and disorientation of the leadership would begin to recede into the background, while the courage of an individual gained weight. Time and time again, they stated that with military operations unfolding in their home country, soldiers would defend their native land, displaying miracles of heroism that would counterbalance the weakness of the entire army. The optimism that grew on this basis was spreading, preparing people for a breakthrough, a counterattack. There were new non-standard ideas, proposals that were met with scepticism by some who did not find them helpful in overcoming the sense of doom, while others welcomed them as a confirmation of their belief in victory, being distracted from reality.

These are the memoirs of Albert Speer, Reich Minister for Armaments and Ammunition of Germany, describing the events of the spring of 1945.[102]

CHAPTER 5

DOES CULTURAL MATRIX SUPPORT ECONOMIC GROWTH (IN BELARUS)?

The question raised in the title of this chapter is rather classical, and it has been in the center of some social researches already. [103] But here it reveals the need to decode the Belarusian cultural matrix. If there is high public demand for the factors that push economic growth, then the cultural matrix with all its roots and features fits into the economy, and the Belarusian behavioral economy is a self-sufficient and successful one. If there is low, or no, public demand for economic growth factors in the country, then the Belarusian cultural matrix needs to be decoded.

To answer this question, three directions were used for evaluation.

First – public demand for structural economic reforms. These reforms are the typical source of economic growth in such transition economies, like Belarus.

Second – public attitude to innovations and technological changes in emerging economies to bring high-tech dividends, to accelerate economic growth.

Third – public need for democracy as the proof of the upper level of societal development and conscious demand for high economic development.

These three groups of factors not only stimulate economic growth, but as it was found, they also push through the channel out of 'middle-income trap' faced by the Belarusian economy.[104]

In order to evaluate Belarusian public reaction to these three directions, six sociological surveys were made. Research Center IPM arranged opinion polls of 1000 respondents in 2006, 1527 respondents in 2008, and 1016 respondents in 2018. The Institute of Sociology of the National Academy of Science made sociological surveys of 1495 respondents in 2014, 1502 respondents in the spring of 2016, and 2086 respondents in the winter of 2016.

Structural Economic Reforms

Structural economic reforms also known as 'supply-side reforms' mean deregulation, price liberalization, increase of competition, privatization, and bankruptcy of insufficient enterprises (usually state-owned enterprises). At the end, all these lead to a change of structure in the national economy: increasing the share of services and ICT, and decreasing the share of agriculture and industry. Due to the Belarusian cultural matrix, industries are not determined by the invisible hand of the market, but by the visible hand of the state using behavioral incentives. So the government chose national champions and industries to support. But this political choice should at least be backed by public opinion.

In an opinion poll, 2014 Belarusians were asked the question: "Which industries need to be developed in the forthcoming 10 – 15 years?" The most popular answer was house construction (50.8% respondents). Belarusians also quite frequently named the export-oriented industries (38%), high-tech agriculture and food production (36.2%), and infrastructure development (31.2%). Although most valuable for economic growth industries like machinery, services and human development were not very popular among Belarusians. 30.6% respondents named machinery, 20.8% noted services, and 19.1% named 'human capital' development.

As Belarusians don't choose industries with the highest added value as the most appropriate for economic growth, it's better to evaluate public demand looking at general economic reforms, rather than on the development of concrete industries. Otherwise, we see that the highest public demand in Belarus is for the industry which is most sensitive for people; house construction (but it is not the most sensitive for the economy, which needs high value added industries, like manufacturing and ICT).

One of the ways to check the public demand for economic reforms is focusing not on the choice of concrete industries, but on the sense of market reforms, using for example, the methodology of the European Bank for Reconstruction and Development.[105] It consists of 11 reform directions: big size privatization, small size privatization, restructuring of enterprises, price liberalization, foreign trade and monetary systems, competition, banking systems, the stock exchange, infrastructure, the labor market, and land ownership. In this regard, a sociological survey may include questions about the general public's attitude to market reforms and government regulations.

According to the opinion polls, the share of market reform supporters increased significantly, to 45.2% by 2018, but it's still lower than the share of government regulation supporters – 49.2% of respondents (Figure 1). Public demand for market reforms was 33.5% of respondents in 2006. Then it decreased to 25.5% by 2008, probably due to global financial crises, the influence of Russian default, and the devaluation of Russian rouble.

Figure 1: Sociological surveys for economic reform supporters in 2006, 2008, 2018, % of respondents[106]

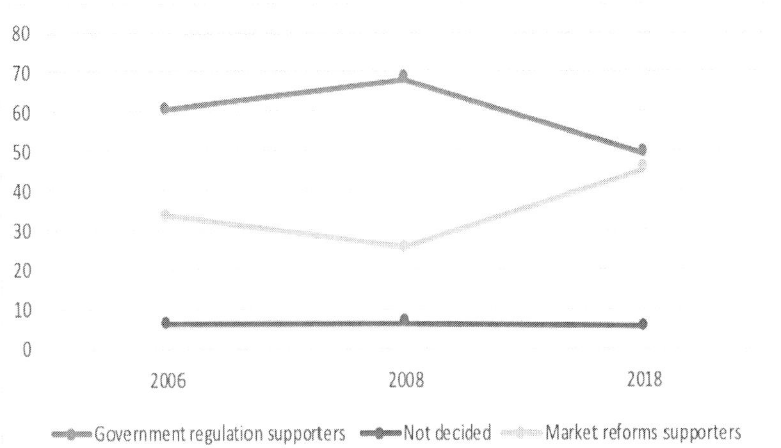

A link was established between the level of education of Belarusians and their support for market reform: a Pearson correlation coefficient is 0.112. The number of market reform supporters increases with the rise of education levels (Figure 2). As an example, the share of market reform supporters with a doctoral degree is 80%, versus 20% of state regulations supporters with a doctoral degree. The ratio of market reform and government supporters with university degrees, but without Doctoral degrees, is, relevantly, 49% and 46%. This trend is also confirmed by a survey of the Institute of Sociology of the National Academy of Science of Belarus. That Institute got the following results in 2016: The share of economic reform supporters with the lowest level of education (who had not finished middle school) was 41.9%. The share of market reform supporters who had graduated from middle school was 57.1%, and the share of reform supporters who were at, or had finished, University was 64.1%.

Figure 2: The links between the level of education and support for economic reform in 2006, 2008, 2018, % of respondents[107]

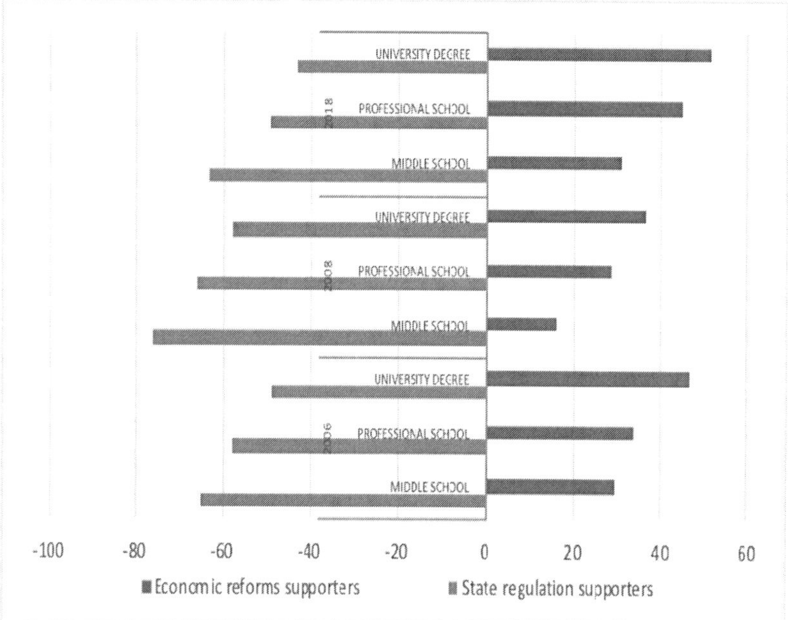

The link is also established between the level of income of Belarusians and their support for market reform: a Pearson correlation coefficient is 0.086. Figure 3 shows the fall in the difference of views between respondents on market reform with upper and lower levels of income in 2006 and in 2018. The Institute of Sociology also proved that in 2016. The higher the level of income of respondents, the higher the support for a market economy. 76.1% of the poor respondents support market economy. 77.2% of middle-income respondents backed reforms, and 80.3% of people with a good income were for economic reform.

Figure 3: The ratios of economic reform supporters with different income levels in 2006, 2008, 2018, % of respondents[108]

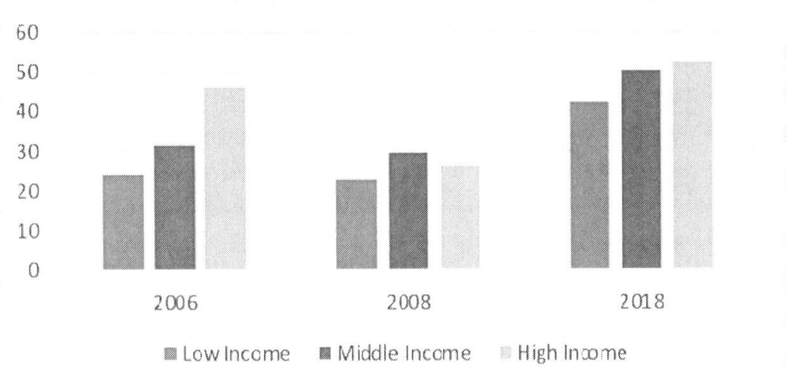

The results of the abovementioned surveys, which showed that the higher level of education the stronger support for economic reform, were double-checked on respondents from urban and rural areas. The fact is that the urban residents have a higher level of education than rural residents. For example, in 2015, the share of rural residents with a University degree was 12.1%, but the share of urban residents who had graduated from University was 28.1%. Similar ratios were seen among rural and urban Belarusians with middle school degrees – 31% and 50.2%. Besides, the income of urban residents was 35% higher than that of rural residents of the country. So, the conclusion previously made was confirmed by the 2016 survey made by the National Academy of Science of Belarus, which showed that urban residents were more reform-oriented than rural residents: 57.7% versus 47.2%.

Innovations and Technological Development

There are two ways to check public demand for innovations and technological development.

First – the indirect way through FDI. The main source of innovations in transition economies is FDI. If the Belarusian public has a friendly attitude towards foreign investors, it could be a good chance to attract innovations in the country.

In 2016, less than half of Belarusians (42.9%) had a friendly attitude to foreign investors. 33.9% of respondents didn't have any opinion on FDI. 12.9% of Belarusians had a consumerist attitude toward foreign investors, and 10.9% of respondents treated FDI as a threat to the Belarusian economy. There is a link between the good attitude of respondents and their level of education. The higher the level of education, the more clear and more positive the attitude to FDI is, and the lower the level of consumerist feelings toward foreign investors. It's important to mention that no linkage is determined between the level of education and a negative attitude to FDI. The most positive feelings towards foreign investors were among those respondents who lived in the cities and thought of themselves as a middle class. So there was a relatively lower public demand for FDI in rural areas and among poor and rich respondents.

Second – the direct way. If we don't connect innovations with FDI it's easier to find bigger and clearer Belarusian support for technology development. According to an IPM Research center survey, there are more respondents in the country who support innovation than there are those who don't. The majority of respondents pointed out that technological development would provide more opportunities for the new generation, and make life easier, more comfortable and healthy. A positive attitude to innovations was also confirmed by a 2016 survey made by the Institute of Sociology of National Academy of Science. More than 70% of respondents were positive that financial investments in innovations would have a high rate of return in the future.

There is a dependence between the attitude to innovations and technological development and the level of education of respondents (Figure 4). The higher the education level, the less people agree with negative sentences about innovations, and they more frequently they use technology in everyday life. There is also a direct linkage between the level of education and financial support for innovations. 70% of respondents with a primary school degree supported the financing of innovations, 72.2% of respondents with middle school degree did so, 76.3% of those with a professional school degree, and 86% of Belarusians who had graduated (or had not finished) from University.

Figure 4: The link between level of education and attitude to innovations and technology development, % of respondents[109]

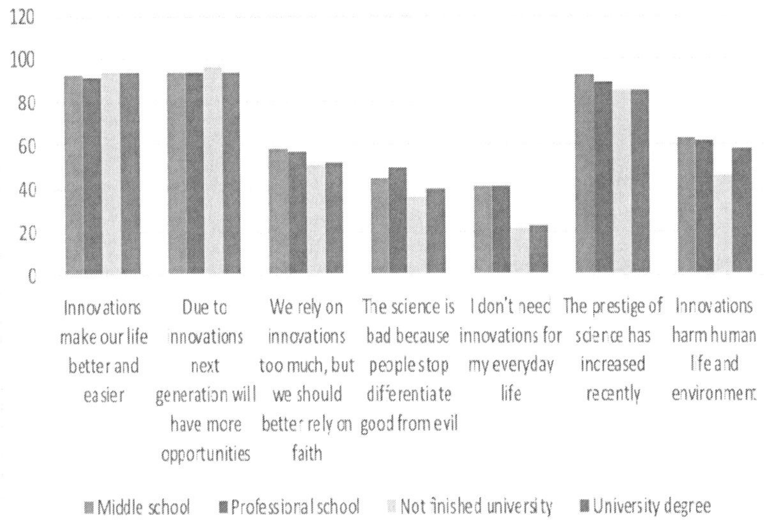

The link is also determined between the attitude toward innovation and the level of income of respondents. The higher the income, the more positive the attitude towards technological development (Figure 5). This trend was also seen in the 2016 survey made by the Institute of Sociology. 69.8% of respondents who considered themselves poor supported the financing of innovation. 74% of Belarusians who thought of themselves as a middle-income class supported the financing of technological development, and 79.2% of respondents with good income supported innovation financing. Surprisingly, there was no big difference between rural and urban supporters of innovation in Belarus – 73.1% and 76.3% relatively.

Figure 5: The link between level of income and attitude to innovations and technology development, % of respondents[110]

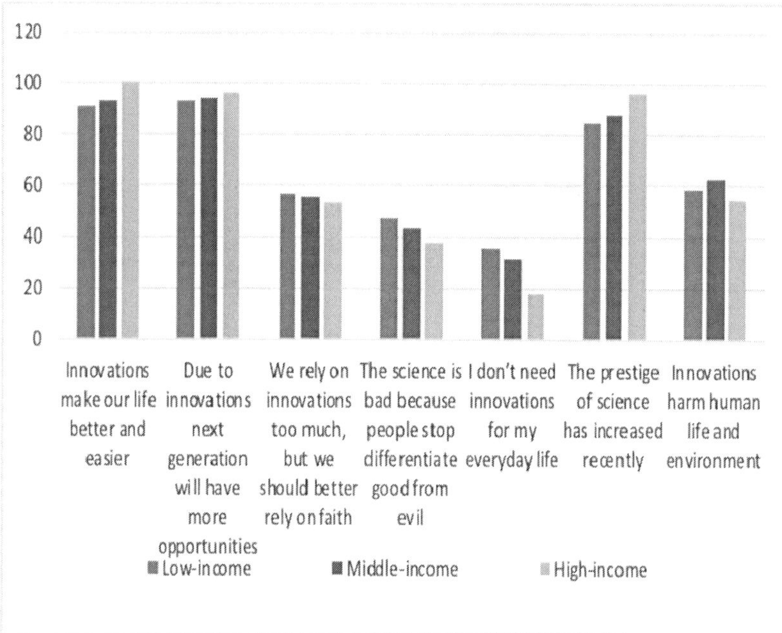

Democracy Development

The evaluation of democracy development by opinion polls sometimes gives controversial results. For example, almost half of the respondents from developing countries understand democracy as the power of military forces and the secret service over an incompetent government, or the power of a religious leader over the national law. They also treat freedom as equal rights and keeping the peace.[111]

According to a survey of 95 countries in the framework of the World and European Values Studies (WVS, EVS) for the period from 1995 to 2005, Belarus (along with the Czech Republic and Slovenia) was one of the countries with the highest level of scepticism regarding power, religion, nationality, and social norms. At the same time, Belarus demonstrated low rates of aspiration regarding freedom of choice and equal opportunities.[112] This points towards the disunity, apathy, and indifference of Belarusians — "We don't need anything: either freedom, or lack of freedom".

Belarusian Research center IPM found linkages in their 2016 survey. The higher the level of education of Belarusians, the higher their support for democracy development and human rights (no matter how they understand that). 56.5% of respondents with a primary school degree supported democracy development, and 61.4% of respondents with a middle school degree. 70.5% of Belarusians who hadn't finished university supported democracy.

The interesting observation was that when respondents started thinking of themselves as people with high incomes, they rapidly increased the demand for democracy. The shares of supporters of democracy development in the group of low and middle income were 63.1% and 63.2% respectively. But the share of respondents with high incomes who supported democracy was much higher, at 84.2%. There was also a difference in support of democracy development between urban and rural residents: 62.9% versus 57.9% respectively.

Even if Belarusians support the idea of democracy development, it's equally important that they trust how this idea is implemented. The questions about the level of trust for the government can help to clarify that, and we can see that the general level of trust went down in Belarus during the decade from 2008 to 2018. Sometimes it's typical for many post-Soviet countries.[113] Moreover, in different cases (for example, Russia) trust in governance becomes crucial for economic growth.[114]

However, there were some indicators of Belarus' governance which were improved, like fighting against criminals, social security, and free medical services (Figure 6). It was also determined that in both 2008 and 2018, respondents with higher income were more satisfied with government efforts.

Figure 6: Satisfaction of government efforts in 2008 and 2018, % of respondents[115]

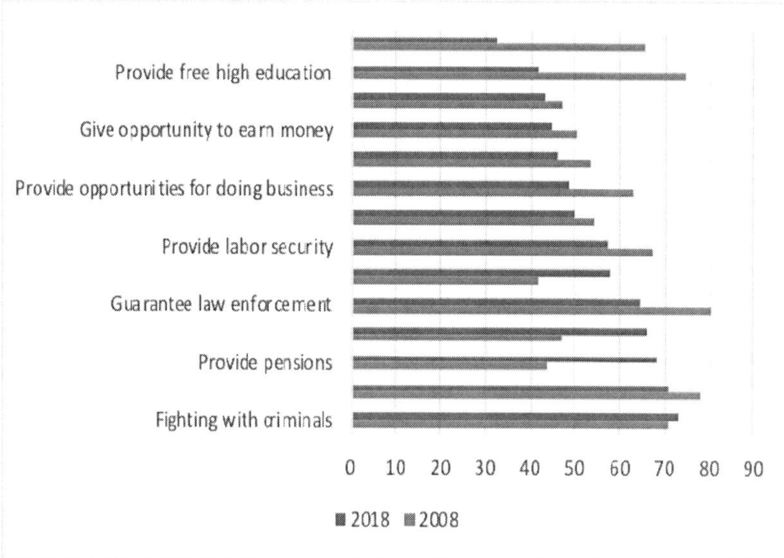

So, in order to answer the question from the title of this chapter "does the cultural matrix support economic growth?" three directions were researched: economic reforms, innovation, and democracy. Which direction has more value for respondents? A 2014 sociological survey by the National Academy of Science provided the answer. After analyses of the responses (see Table 1), we can conclude that the biggest public demand in Belarus was for innovation and technological development, the second level of demand was for democracy development, and the last one was for economic reforms.

Table 1: Public expectations in Belarus, % of respondents[116][117]

Responses	How do you see Belarus in 10 – 15 years?		
	Country with innovations and highly developed technologies	Country with developed democracy and law enforcement	Country with reformed economy, developed finance and financial markets
It's rather real	44.5	41.2	34.4
It's possible, but not highly probable	31.6	28.4	31.7
It's unreal	7.6	7.7	11.0
Not sure	14.3	19.6	20.8

So, the answer to the above mentioned question is **"No!"** The current Belarusian cultural matrix doesn't have economic reform as its priority and doesn't directly support economic growth, other than through innovations and democracy development. That's why the cultural matrix needs to be decoded in Belarus in order to push forward economic growth.

How can the Belarusian cultural matrix be decoded to make it more economy oriented? It has been determined that public demand for economic growth has its elasticity in Belarus (Table 2). The income indicator shows the highest level of elasticity. The higher the level of income of respondents, the higher public demand for all three directions to support economic growth is. The lowest level of elasticity is urbanization. The most sensitive issue for public demand, across different levels of education, income, and urbanization, is the direction of innovation and technology development. Two directions of economic reform and democracy development are less reflective of public demand.

Table 2: Elasticity of public demand for economic reforms, innovations and democracy development depending on the level of income, education and urbanization, 2016[118].

	Growth of public demand on innovations, %	Growth of public demand on economic reforms, %	Growth of public demand on democracy development, %
1%-growth of the number of respondents with high level of income	4.0	3.2	2.5
1%-growth of the number of respondents with not finished high education and graduated from University	3.1	1.4	1.9
1%-growth of the number of urban residents	0.7	0.3	0.4

After the evaluation of public demand and its elasticity, it's easy to make the conclusion that *public support for economic growth in Belarus depends on the level of income of respondents.* The higher the income of the respondents, the higher their support for economic growth. As there are a lot of poor and middle-income respondents in Belarus, there is little demand for economic reforms, innovation or democracy. This conclusion is also supported by other research.[119][120] These prove that when incomes rise, so, too, does cognitive capacity. And the failure of the poor is part and parcel of the misfortune of being poor in the first place.

How can people's income be increased, if it all looks like it is moving in a circle? The way to break the circle and to decode economic behavior is to use FDI. They will bring not only higher incomes, but also different and more suitable values for the long-term public support of economic growth in Belarus.

CHAPTER 6

ECONOMIC DECODING OF THE CULTURAL MATRIX

At one of his public lectures delivered in 2014 in Ukraine, where he attracted a house capacity akin to that of a rock star, Kakha Bendukidze, former Minister for the Reform Coordination of Georgia, a businessman and statesman, spoke about his standard approach for assessing the investment climate. "It takes only a few seconds. You can feel as soon as the plane lands and you step out. You can tell right away whether or not it is possible to do business here".

Having pondered his words for several years while visiting different countries and regions, I intended to prove or disprove his claims. I registered my feelings automatically upon the first moments of arrival. And every time, I saw that Kakha Bendukidze was right. We instantly get our first impression of a country at the airport, and then it grows stronger and stronger every minute, hour, day, and year, remaining practically unchanged. This instantaneous assessment obtained from a random glance, ambient noise, gesture, accidental contact, is made up of a thousand little things. People around us, the clothes they wear, their faces, manners, walking pace, airport workload, the faces of passport control officers, the presence of identifiable global brands in shops and restaurants. And the one thing that is very revealing and haunting as you walk around the airport is advertising. What do they advertise at your city's airport? In Shanghai it is real estate, while in Beijing there are air pollution masks. In Cyprus there are binary options, in Vienna, airline companies and banks, while in Paris, it is hotels and tourism. In Moscow, there are Russian cuisine restaurants and vodka, and in Minsk, casinos. In Ho Chi Minh City, the billboards say, "Your ad could be here". All this is part of the investment climate. It is a magnetic field to attract foreign investors.

The Way of Decoding of the Cultural Matrix is to Attract FDI

Foreign investors are adventurous and sceptical, apolitical and pragmatic, cynical and romantic, and they are a direct channel for the fast transfer of managerial, financial, technological, cultural, and other values. Neither bilateral trade nor loans, neither culture nor education, can ensure the level of interpenetration and mutual trust that investments can. When a foreign investor comes to a country, he naturally shares with it his most valuable asset – his experience - as well as all his own, and the country's, risks. If we compare the lender and the investor, the lender is always more conservative, more risk averse, and focused on getting his investment back with a moderate profit. By contrast, the investor plays the 'long game'. He is constantly exposed to risk, seeking opportunities, and focused on investment multiplication rather than savings. This provides an economic impetus to ensure the growth of the economy. Mutual magnetism of the cultural matrices, matching values and mentality, and synchronised unconscious behaviour, are needed to attract this type of investor. Basically, foreign investors facilitate, through their mediation, the integration of the national and global matrices.

A number of studies confirm the stimulating effect of foreign direct investment on economic growth, which materialises under certain conditions.

For instance, the strongest effect of foreign direct investment on economic growth is registered if the economy is export-oriented and open for foreign trade.[121] There are also records of economic growth boosted through foreign direct investment if the recipient country has a sufficiently high level of technology.[122] In turn, foreign investors typically bring new technologies to be applied, given that there is a sufficient level of human development to be able to use such technologies in the country.[123] Surprisingly, recent studies proved that tax benefits didn't attract FDI or stimulate economic growth.[124]

Evidence from 94 developing countries over the period 1984-2009 has revealed that another means of promoting economic growth is the quality of institutions in the recipient countries. This attracts foreign direct investment that, in turn, boosts economic growth.[125] Evidence from local companies from 17 transition economies for the period 2002-2005 has demonstrated a positive effect on their productivity, generated by foreign direct investment.[126] Evidence from different regions of Russia has determined one more factor for attracting foreign direct investments which boost economic growth – the quality of public administration. If the level of public administration improves from medium to high, then foreign direct investments increase by 158%.[127]

Investments Reversal in Belarus

I wish I could say that the measures taken over many years to improve the attractiveness of Belarus' investment climate generate a positive effect. This is supposedly illustrated by the annual improvement of the country's ranking in the Doing Business Report, shown in recent years as holding 63rd position in 2014; 57th in 2015; 44th in 2016; and 37th in 2017; 38th in 2018; 37th in 2019; 49th in 2020.[128] However, the improved ranking seems to satisfy the developers of the ranking methodology, as well as those who have acquired expertise and learned to adjust to it, rather than the demand from businesses, because the truth is that it was in these years that an unexpected reversal of investment commenced in Belarus. In other words, the ranking and its methodology do not reflect the true investor sentiment. The investment climate becomes similar to a clean and nice city being abandoned by its residents. The reversal of investment in Belarus can be tracked through a range of indicators.

The decline in the inflow of net foreign direct investment. According to the National Statistical Committee of the Republic of Belarus, net foreign direct investments totalled USD 1,948 million in 2013; USD 1,558 million in 2014; USD 1,516 million in 2015; and USD 1,307 million in 2016.[129] An assessment of the foreign direct investment stock accumulated over a long period of time shows that Belarus' performance is lower than that of other countries. For instance, if we take the period of the last 16 years, the foreign direct investments in Belarus had reached USD 1,968 per capita as of 1 October 2016. To put this in perspective, they amounted to USD 2,760 per capita in Russia, USD 7,887 in Kazakhstan, and USD 15,251 in the EU.

The net closure of foreign-invested organisations. Since 2015, more foreign-invested organisations have been closed than established in Belarus (Figure 7). Moreover, the number of foreign-invested organisations went down in all regions of Belarus in 2016 compared to 2015. This reveals systemic rather than regional problems.

Figure 7. Number of joint ventures and foreign enterprises in Belarus, 2011 – Q1 2016.[130]

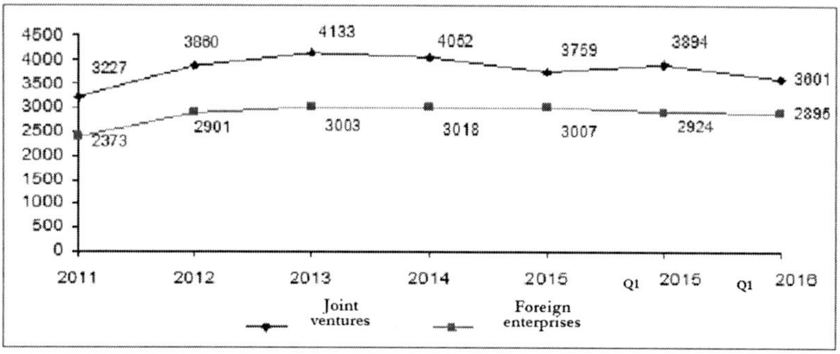

The declining authorised funds of foreign organisations. The authorised funds of foreign-invested enterprises have also been declining since 2015 (Figure 8). The regional breakdown of these funds demonstrates an outflow of foreign capital from every oblast of Belarus (except for Vitebsk oblast) and the city of Minsk.

Figure 8. Contributions to the authorised funds of joint ventures and foreign enterprises, 2011 – Q1 2016, million USD.[131]

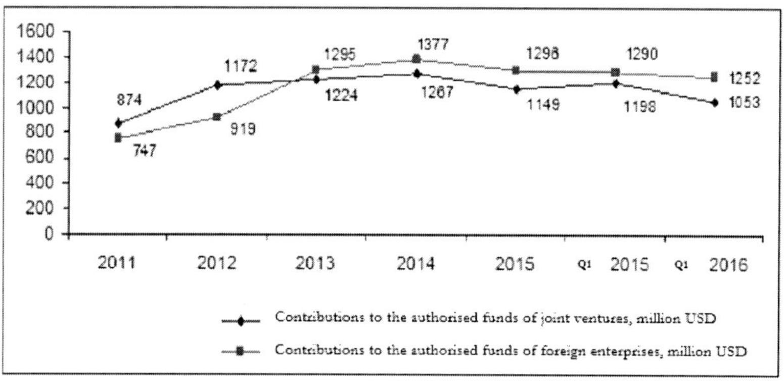

The reasons for the investments reversal

The weakening payable demand in Belarus. The decline in output, GDP, real incomes of the population, and payable demand, are the key factors affecting investor sentiment. In 2015, real incomes and consumption dropped respectively by 5.9% and 3.6%. In addition, investment climate deterioration could be associated with lower labour productivity, which fell in general in Belarus by 28% in USD terms in 2015. It is noteworthy that, when choosing Belarus as a financial investment target, while foreign investors do assess sovereign risks and opportunities, they focus more on regional ones, due to the interdependence of the countries in the region. For instance, according to the Ministry of Economy of Belarus, a deceleration of economic growth in Russia by 1% triggers a drop in Belarus' economic growth rate by 0.8-0.9%. In this regard, the clouded outlook for Russia's economy deters foreign investors from Belarus.

The repayment of external loans by foreign investors. Unlike Belarusian state-owned enterprises, which were able to restructure their external loans in 2015 owing to government support, foreign organisations were obliged to repay loans on their own. This has reduced the size of reinvested profits and generally resulted in capital outflows. The repayment of loans may explain the capital outflows from developing countries, which recommenced in 2014, for the first time since 1978, and exceeded USD 700 billion in 2015.[132]

The dropping profits. Reinvested profits are a major source of foreign direct investment in Belarus. The deterioration in the financial condition of foreign-invested organisations in 2014-2015 resulted in lower reinvested profits. The share of profitable foreign-invested organisations in the total number of foreign enterprises in Belarus dropped from 80.9% in 2013, to 63.8% in 2014, and 66.5% in 2015. This trend is also global in nature for foreign investors. For instance, critics in China point out that Chinese direct investments are often oriented to countries, "where there is no order", and this would not pay off. In this regard, Chinese investors focus more and more often on developed countries. London emerges as the European centre for Chinese financial investments, Germany for technological investments (following the high-profile purchase of Kuka, the German robot manufacturer, by the Chinese company Midea). Canada is to play a similar role in the Americas.

The de-dollarization of authorised funds launched in 2015. Since that year, the authorised funds of joint ventures and foreign enterprises in reorganisation have been recalculated and formed in the national currency. In view of the depreciation processes and statistical processing of authorised funds in USD, the total amount of authorised funds of foreign-invested organisations has decreased. At the same time, this factor should not be overestimated, since, as noted above, the direct replenishment of authorised funds is only 2% of total foreign direct investments on a net basis.

Belarus' loss of its market share in Russia. The argument that investing in Belarus ensures access to the Russian market is increasingly being called into question, given the recurrent political tensions between Belarus and Russia. On the whole, the trade share of Belarus in the Russian market has dropped significantly in recent years. Whereas in 2000 Belarus' share in Russian imports accounted for 11%, it became 4.7% in 2011, and 4% in 2014. In turn, the share of the EU countries increased from 33% in 2000 to 42% in 2011, and up to 48% in 2014. The new Russian policies of sanctions, counter-sanctions, isolation, and import substitution, do not improve the situation.

The mounting pressure on the economy. In 2015, some evident coercive pressure on the economy (in particular on foreign investors) emerged in the form of an increased number of court cases dealing with administrative offenses in the economic sphere. According to the Supreme Court, the number of cases increased from 9,792 in 2015 to 13,361 in 2014. Along with that, the major contributors to the coercive pressure on the national economy in 2014 and 2015 were the Ministry of Taxes and Duties – correspondingly 6,804 and 9,060 cases, the State Customs Committee – 466 and 651 cases, the Ministry of Internal Affairs – 446 and 415 cases, and the State Control Committee – 357 and 398 cases.

In addition, there has been a rise in the ratio of cases resulting in administrative penalties to the overall number of cases filed in court: a total of 0.88 in 2014 and 0.9 in 2015, including cases related to the Ministry of Taxes and Duties – 0.91 and 0.92, the State Control Committee – 0.85 and 0.88, the State Customs Committee – 0.47 and 0.73, and the Ministry of Internal Affairs – 0.69 and 0.66. Only a few appeals were satisfied in whole, or in part, against the action or inaction of officials and verification of legality. Moreover, the number of appeals has been decreasing since 2013. 102 decisions were challenged in court as appeals against actions of officials of the Ministry of Taxes and Duties in 2013; 12 claims were satisfied in whole or in part; in 2015 the corresponding figures were 78 and 6. Regarding the State Customs Committee, the numbers were 168 and 78 in 2013, and 112 and 6 in 2015.

A year-long comparison of the overall quantity of initiated criminal cases related to economic offences shows a steady increase in number: 2,129 cases in 2012, 2,639 in 2013, 2,867 in 2014, and 3,580 in 2015. The number of administrative cases related to economic offences has also been growing: 111,421 cases in 2012, 121,052 in 2013, 121,371 in 2014, and 128,005 in 2015.

The accumulated risks of termination of investment contracts. 1,926 investment contracts, with a declared investment amount of USD 40.2 billion, were concluded in Belarus during 2009-2016. Of those, 447 contracts totalling USD 2.8 billion have been implemented, while 878 contracts (45%) totalling USD 15.7 billion have been terminated. The remaining projects are underway. The primary cause of investment contract termination is the investors' failure to comply with commitments that have turned out to be burdensome. Taking into account an empirically high probability of investment contract breach and termination, this risk is accumulated, and reaches its critical level, affecting the decisions of new investors.

The built-up negative international image. Sanctions and long-term political isolation create a biased attitude to Belarus among foreign investors, and it is usually some emotional dislike rather than their rational economic sentiment. Regular investment forums aimed at promoting the Belarusian investment climate are sometimes not comparable to one or several reports in prestigious business publications. For instance, in the international bestseller *Industries of the Future*, by Alec Ross, Advisor for Information and Communication Technologies to Hillary Clinton, Belarus is referred to as an example of an unattractive investment climate, and an underdeveloped ICT sector, and it is contrasted with Estonia with its e-government and openness to innovations.[133] Another popular business publication *The End of the Free Market,* by American economist Ian Bremmer, puts Belarus in the same league as the economies of North Korea, Cuba, and Myanmar.[134]

The regional instability since 2014. The military conflict in Ukraine, and the political confrontation between Russia and the West, are developments which have projected investment risks onto Belarus. It is not even a matter of the risk of a military conflict on Belarusian territory. Curiously enough, even the name Belarus (Byelorussia, White Russia, and other translations used in foreign languages) sometimes triggers alarming associations with Russia among foreign investors. The problem may be more sweeping when an investor sees Belarus as part of Russia, and this conditions his attitude. For instance, associations with country names that sound similar sometimes become the source of stereotypical attitudes among investors towards toponyms ending in '-stan': Afghanistan, Kazakhstan, Tajikistan, Turkmenistan, Uzbekistan, etc. Several studies of investor psychology indicate that companies are more likely to attract investment if they have pleasant sounding names rather than promising financial statements.[135]

The Need for FDI in Belarus

The unexpected reversal of foreign investments out of Belarus elicits a defensive emotional reaction to just wave it away. The orientation towards the Soviet past compels a reliance on oneself. Some internal doubts arise: "Is there such a need for foreign investments in Belarus?" But, when you think about it, the answer is that they are not only useful for cultural decoding, but also relevant for addressing economic challenges.

First of all, *foreign investments are essential to restore and sustain economic growth in Belarus.* According to the Economy Research Institute of the Ministry of Economy of Belarus, USD 9.3-9.6 billion of foreign direct investments are to be mobilised in 2016-2020 on a net basis to attain GDP growth of 10-15% over the five years (2-3% per year). Approximately the same amount is needed to bring the gold and foreign currency reserves up to a safe level. Even in view of the potential decline in imports, foreign direct investments in the amount of about USD 10 billion would be needed to hold the gold and foreign currency reserves above the critical level of three months of imports. Based on IMF methodology, as of 1 January 2017, the international reserve assets amounted to about USD 5 billion, of which liquid reserve assets in foreign exchange were USD 2.4 billion. If we take into account the need for non-debt financing of foreign currency debt, the required amount of foreign direct investment would grow even larger. With further refinancing of foreign currency loans with new borrowings, peaks of foreign exchange payments may remain for a period of several years, averaging at about USD 3 billion a year. This would constrain economic growth. Therefore, the amount of foreign direct investment required for 2016-2020, to ensure some moderate economic growth, as well as monetary and debt security in Belarus, exceeds USD 30 billion.

Second, *attracting foreign direct investment would help improve the state-owned corporate sector and save the budget funds that are currently allocated to support it.* In addition to the obvious need for technology transfer, mobilisation of management skills, and creation of highly productive jobs, the financial rehabilitation of state-owned enterprises is high on today's agenda. For instance, in 2015, the organisations subordinated to the Ministry of Industry received government support in the amount of about BYR 10 trillion and completed the reporting period with a net loss of BYR 10 trillion and overdue accounts receivable of over BYR 10 trillion. Despite this unprecedented government support, the contribution of the organisations under the Ministry of Industry to GDP was less than 3% in 2015; their output dropped by 24.5%, exports by 35%, and one third of their workers (64.5 thousand out of 180 thousand) faced involuntary part-time employment.

In addition, in December 2015, the production capacity utilisation rate in industry averaged 58%, including automotive enterprises, where this indicator was 40%. Mobilisation of foreign investment in the authorised funds of commercial organisations subordinated to the Ministry of Industry would help reduce the government support provided to these enterprises and reallocate the budget resources to more productive expenditures, such as science and education. For instance, in 2015, budget expenditures related to organisations under the Ministry of Industry — mainly in the form of budget loans —amounted to BYR 9.9 trillion. This compares to BYR 9.2 trillion allocated to defence, BYR 7 trillion to education, BYR 6.3 trillion to healthcare, BYR 5.4 trillion to finance the state apparatus, and BYR 1.9 trillion to science.

Thus, foreign direct investments are essential nowadays, not so much for securing growth, as for safeguarding the gains in social and economic development and ensuring Belarus' economic security. Along with the unexpected investment reversal, several specific aspects of the Belarusian investment climate could also be highlighted: a high concentration of investments at a few sites, entities and countries, as well as the focus of foreign investors on loss minimisation rather than profit maximisation.

The following trends are clearly indicative of foreign investment concentration:

- *the reliance primarily on two investor countries – Russia and Cyprus* (Figure 9). In 2015, they accounted for 54.8% of total foreign direct investment. Moreover, many foreign companies reach Belarus via Cyprus to optimise their tax payments, and via Russia to benefit from the simpler registration procedure. Besides, in both cases these may be Belarusian companies, reinvesting in Belarus via Russia and Cyprus to conceal the origin of their financial resources;

Figure 9. Share of investor countries in total net foreign direct investment in Belarus, 2011-2015, %[136].

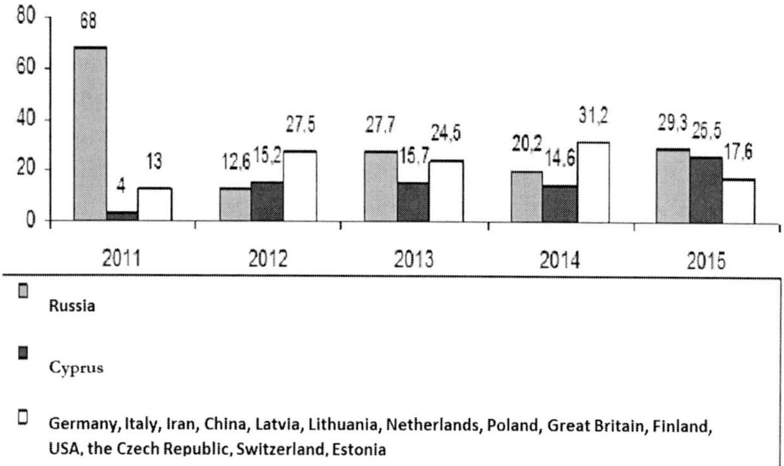

- *the high concentration of foreign direct investment on a few corporate investors.* In 2011-2015, the five largest foreign investors, *inter alia* Kronospan, Heineken, and Stadler, accounted for 40% of foreign capital investment in authorised funds, with one investor accounting for over 20%. As for reinvested profits, over the past five-year period, the five largest re-investors, *inter alia* MTS, EPAM, and Mozyr Oil Refinery, accounted for 26% of total reinvested profits, with one investor accounting for about 10%; and

- *the financial concentration of foreign investors on large enterprises is an indication of the insignificant number of attractive investment projects in Belarus.* 1% of organisations with an authorised fund of over USD 5 million account for 65% of total net foreign direct investments. By contrast, 99% of foreign-invested organisations in Belarus are enterprises with an authorised fund of up to USD 5 million, hosting only 35% of total net foreign direct investment.

The unexpected and untimely investment reversal, unsustainable concentration of investments, investors' focus on loss minimisation – all these factors impair the long-term economic growth potential. However, the protracted economic crisis has inevitable social consequences. A rise in unemployment by 1% is estimated to result in an increase in the suicide rate by 1.3%.[137]

With due account for the debt and budget constraints, there seems to be no visible option other than opening up the economy to foreign direct investment to restore economic growth and maintain social stability. Under the pressure of the instinct to survive, the Belarusian cultural matrix must change and become more attractive for foreign investors. It may be necessary to modify at least those features that influence the investment climate. For instance, doublethink and orientation towards the Soviet past, along with privatisation restraint, discourage foreign investors and create conditions for investment reversal. Orientation to scale fosters focusing on a few countries and investing corporations, which increases dependence on the performance of just a few large investment projects. Paternalism and the corresponding public-private partnership led to investors' orientation to loss minimisation rather than risk-taking and profit maximisation. In light of the foregoing, the socio-cultural environment increasingly affects the investment climate. For this reason, the attitude of the Belarusian society towards foreign investors merits separate study.

Belarusians' Attitude towards Foreign Investors

A sociological study, based on the country-wide survey of 2016, was conducted to assess the attitude of Belarusians towards foreign investors. The sample covered 2,086 respondents and was representative by gender, age, education, regions, and types of settlement. In the framework of the survey, emphasis was placed on the attitude of Belarusians towards foreign investors, their vision of advantages and risks related to attracting foreign direct investment in Belarus.

In general, the Belarusian population is quite well disposed towards foreign investors. The biggest proportion of respondents (42.9%) considers foreign investors as partners for the country. They think that everyone would benefit from this partnership based on mutual interests. 12.8% believe that foreign investors can, and must, be used for the benefit of the national economy as a 'cash cow'. 10.9% consider foreign investors as a threat to the economic stability and security, and think that it is better to develop the Belarusian economy without foreign investments. It should be noted that the second largest group of respondents does not have a clear view of foreign investors, and this is the target group for encoding a different set of values.

When assessing the advantages and disadvantages of foreign investments, respondents acknowledge that the overall balance is positive.

The potential positive implications that Belarusians see in mobilising foreign investment include new jobs (32.3%), new advanced technologies (24.5%), access to external markets and an increase in exports (23.5%). The major risk most frequently stressed by respondents (19.6%) is the crowding out of domestic producers from the market. A high proportion of respondents (32.8%) also found it difficult to answer this question (Figure 10).

Figure 10. Benefits and risks related to attracting foreign investors and customers for Belarus' economy, 2016, % of respondents[138]

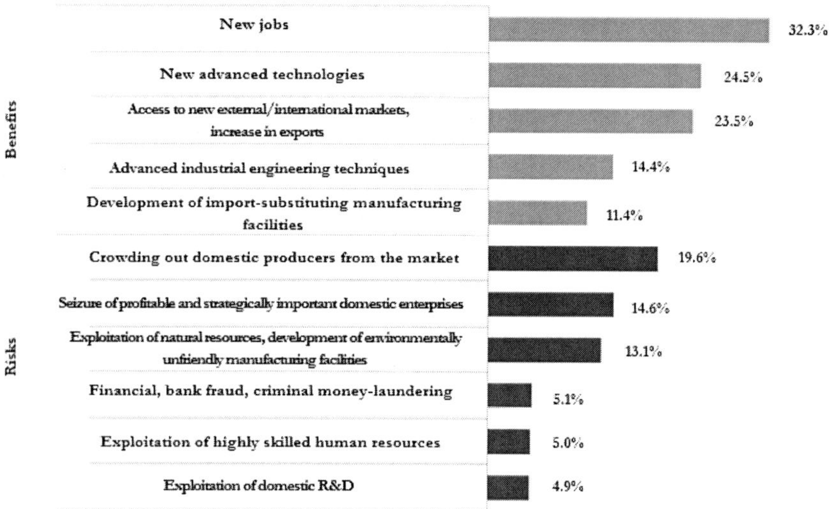

A comparative analysis of Belarusians' attitude towards foreign investors depending on the type of settlement shows that urban residents, more often than not, consider a foreign investor as a partner, as opposed to rural residents (Table 3). In addition, urban residents more often note both the potential benefits of attracting foreign investors and the risks associated with crowding out domestic producers from the market, the seizure of strategically important enterprises, and the exploitation of natural resources (Table 4).

Table 3: Frequency distribution of responses to the question: "Choose the statement that characterises your attitude towards foreign investors …", 2016, % of respondents[139]

Response options	Urban	Rural
A foreign investor is a partner for the country, everyone would benefit from this partnership based on mutual interests	45.7	34.7
A foreign investor is a 'cash cow' that can and must be used for the benefit of the national economy	11.5	16.5
A foreign investor is a threat to economic stability and security, it is better to develop the Belarusian economy without foreign investment	10.1	13.4
Not sure	32.7	35.4

Table 4: Frequency distribution of responses to the question: "What benefits and risks related to attracting foreign investors and customers for Belarus' economy do you see?", 2016, % of respondents[140]

	Response options	Urban	Rural
Benefits	New jobs	32.8	30.8
	New advanced technologies	25.7	21.3
	Access to new external/international markets, increase in exports	24.9	19.7
	Advanced industrial engineering techniques	15.3	11.6
	Development of import-substituting manufacturing facilities	11.7	10.6
Risks	Crowding out domestic producers from the market	20.8	16.1
	Seizure of profitable and strategically important domestic enterprises	15.4	12.4
	Exploitation of natural resources, development of environmentally unfriendly manufacturing facilities	14.4	9.4
	Financial, bank fraud, criminal money-laundering	5.2	4.8
	Exploitation of highly skilled human resources	4.9	5.0
	Exploitation of domestic R&D	4.7	5.5
Not sure		31.5	36.6

Depending on the region of residence, the highest rates of positive attitude towards foreign investors, considered as partners, are registered in Minsk (51.2%), Brest oblast (50.7%) and Vitebsk oblast (49.5%); the lowest rates are in Gomel oblast (25.9%) and Mogilev oblast (32.1%) (Table 5).

Table 5: Frequency distribution of responses to the question: "Choose the statement that describes your attitude towards foreign investors ...", 2016, % of respondents[141]

Response options	Brest oblast	Vitebsk oblast	Gomel oblast	Grodno oblast	Minsk	Minsk oblast	Mogilev oblast
A foreign investor is a partner for the country, everyone would benefit from this partnership based on mutual interests	50.7	49.5	25.9	43.8	51.2	44.4	32.1
A foreign investor is a 'cash cow' that can and must be used for the benefit of the national economy	11.3	3.6	20.5	12.0	13.6	16.3	10.3
A foreign investor is a threat to economic stability and security, it is better to develop the Belarusian economy without foreign investments	10.9	6.2	25.9	8.2	8.0	8.9	6.2
Not sure	27.2	40.7	27.8	36.1	27.2	30.4	51.4

Among the potential benefits, the option of new job creation is the most frequent choice of respondents in Minsk oblast (43.4%) and Minsk (43.2%); access to new international markets in Grodno oblast (37.6%); and new advanced technologies in Minsk oblast (34.4%) and Minsk (32.4%). Residents of Minsk (28.0%), more often than representatives of other regions, mentioned potential crowding out of domestic producers from the market as a risk. Respondents from Brest oblast (21.4%) and Minsk oblast (20.8%) cited the seizure of important domestic enterprises; those from Vitebsk oblast (24.1%) cited exploitation of natural resources and the development of environmentally unfriendly manufacturing facilities (Table 6).

Table 6: Frequency distribution of responses to the question: "What benefits and risks related to attracting foreign investors and customers for Belarus' economy do you see?", 2016, % of respondents[142][143]

	Response options	Brest oblast	Vitebsk oblast	Gomel oblast	Grodno oblast	Minsk	Minsk oblast	Mogilev oblast
Benefits	New jobs	16.7	29.0	21.3	40.3	43.2	43.4	30.5
	New advanced technologies	13.1	25.6	14.0	37.6	33.0	24.8	16.1
	Access to new external/international markets, increase in exports	22.0	23.7	12.9	30.7	32.4	34.4	12.5
	Advanced industrial engineering techniques	17.2	9.9	9.5	13.2	21.3	17.0	8.9
	Development of import-substituting manufacturing facilities	15.3	12.0	8.5	8.2	16.4	10.5	6.3
Risks	Crowding out domestic producers from the market	19.2	19.3	12.3	16.1	28.0	20.5	18.9
	Seizure of profitable and strategically important domestic enterprises	21.4	17.0	4.4	8.7	16.8	20.8	11.0
	Exploitation of natural resources, development of environmentally unfriendly manufacturing facilities	5.1	24.1	6.9	5.9	16.6	19.3	12.4
	Financial, bank fraud, criminal money-laundering	5.6	3.0	2.2	3.2	9.3	5.0	4.4

	Exploitation of highly skilled human resources	3.1	4.6	2.9	2.0	8.1	7.7	4.1
	Exploitation of domestic R&D	3.9	3.0	2.5	3.3	5.8	6.2	11.8
Not sure		40.9	40.5	26.4	32.8	25.0	23.7	46.3

There were no essential differences between males and females in their attitude towards foreign investors. Indicators by gender are broadly in line with national average values. At the same time, males are more confident than females in their positive, as well as negative, assessments of the consequences of foreign investors' entry.

With age, the population's positive attitude towards foreign investors weakens, while their negative attitude strengthens. The middle-aged generation (31-45 years old) demonstrates a more pronounced consumer attitude towards foreign investors. At the same time, the same age category (36.2% of respondents) most clearly formulated their expectations related to foreign investors as the creation of new jobs. These respondents also noted benefits such as access to external markets (29.8%) and new technologies (27.9%) more frequently than others. A correlation between educational attainment and confidence in the formulation of one's attitude towards foreign investors is observed. Respondents with higher educational attainment, as opposed to those with lower educational attainment, display a stronger positive, as well as a stronger negative, attitude towards investors. Respondents with the highest educational attainment very clearly identified the benefits of foreign investors – new jobs (41.6%), new technologies (35.6%), and access to external markets (33.8%) (Tables 7, 8).

Table 7: Frequency distribution of responses to the question: "Choose the statement that describes your attitude towards foreign investors ...", 2016, % of respondents, sample by age and education[144]

	Under the age of 30	31-45 years old	46-60 years old	aged 61 and older	primary + incomplete secondary + general secondary education	vocational technical + secondary vocational education	incomplete higher + higher + postgraduate education
A foreign investor is a partner for the country, everyone would benefit from this partnership based on mutual interests	48.5	46.9	41.0	29.9	36.2	42.6	57.0
A foreign investor is a 'cash cow' that can and must be used for the benefit of the national economy	12.3	14.6	13.7	9.7	13.4	13.4	10.2
A foreign investor is a threat to economic stability and security, it is better to develop the Belarusian economy without foreign investments	8.3	11.1	13.1	11.7	10.6	10.9	11.7
Not sure	30.8	27.4	32.3	48.7	39.7	33.2	21.1

Table 8: Frequency distribution of responses to the question: "What benefits and risks related to attracting foreign investors and customers for Belarus' economy do you see?", 2016, % of respondents, sample by age and education[145]

	under the age of 30	31-45 years old	46-60 years old	aged 61 and older	primary + incomplete secondary + general secondary education	vocational technical + secondary vocational education	incomplete higher + higher + postgraduate education
Crowding out domestic producers from the market	22.1	19.3	19.8	15.4	16.4	20.7	24.0
Access to new external/international markets, increase in exports	24.9	29.8	20.8	16.2	19.3	22.6	33.8
Seizure of profitable and strategically important domestic enterprises	15.3	13.2	17.0	11.4	13.3	14.8	16.5
New advanced technologies	27.8	27.9	23.7	15.2	20.4	23.2	35.6
New jobs	34.2	36.2	32.5	22.9	27.7	32.5	41.6
Development of import-substituting manufacturing facilities	13.1	14.0	10.2	6.8	9.9	11.3	15.0
Advanced industrial engineering techniques	16.4	18.2	12.3	8.6	11.6	12.8	23.5
Financial, bank fraud, criminal money-laundering	5.2	5.2	4.5	5.9	3.8	5.7	6.9
Exploitation of highly skilled human resources	4.0	6.0	5.3	4.0	4.1	5.1	6.5
Exploitation of domestic R&D	4.1	5.6	5.6	4.1	3.9	4.9	7.0

Exploitation of natural resources, development of environmentally unfriendly manufacturing facilities	12.9	11.7	14.6	13.0	11.2	11.9	19.5
Not sure	30.2	28.6	30.0	48.3	40.3	31.6	20.1

Thus, the social groups that produce a positive effect on the investment climate in the Republic of Belarus include residents of urban areas, Brest, Vitebsk, Minsk, and Grodno oblasts, and the city of Minsk, are under the age of 45, and with incomplete or completed higher education, regardless of whether these are males or females. Besides, these groups more clearly express not only positive expectations regarding the benefits associated with foreign investors in the form of new jobs, new technologies, and new external markets, but also fears – crowding out domestic producers from the market, exploitation of natural resources, and the seizure of strategically important enterprises. In turn, residents of rural areas, Gomel and Mogilev oblasts, aged 46 and older, with the lowest level of educational attainment, are among the social groups that cultivate a negative investment climate in Belarus.

The basis for the decoding of the investment climate in Belarus includes: urbanisation, improvement of educational attainment, and targeted work through mass media to raise awareness among the 'age' and 'regional' groups regarding the benefits of foreign investment. At the same time, decoding is still an auxiliary mechanism, when other mechanisms, including economic ones, are put in place. Decoding based merely on statistics, expert appraisal, and surveys of the population may produce a biased effect. In this case, all that can be created is a comfort zone for the population in the context of their perception of foreign investors, but not a comfortable working environment for investors; and this would not induce foreign investments. It also brings to mind the improved *Doing Business* ranking, accompanied by investment reversal. Everyone is happy, including experts, advisers, the government, and the population, but not investors. In this regard, in the process of decoding the Belarusian economy, it is important to rely on surveys of foreign investors[146] to assess the investment climate. In order to move from theoretical to practical decoding Belarus should start with experiment, and the good pilot project to attract FDI is special economic zone.

CHAPTER 7

INDUSTRIAL PARK 'GREAT STONE'

There is a bronze monument to China's reformer – Deng Xiaoping – located on the sightseeing platform of the Lotus Mountain park in Shenzhen. The bronze Deng Xiaoping is heading towards Hong Kong. When I visited it in 2007, the escort team told a story about the city of Shenzhen and how it was constructed purposefully across the river from Hong Kong. The objective was to demonstrate to Hong Kong residents that it is not scary to unite with China, and likewise there is business and development to be found on the opposite bank. In turn, Hong Kong attracted Chinese residents, and in the 1990s and 2000s its success story became the model of effective business management and urban development for almost every large city in China.

When visiting Shenzhen and Hong Kong ten years later, in 2017, I heard stories about residents of Hong Kong more and more often moving to Shenzhen. I saw that the experience of Hong Kong appeared to have expanded to Shanghai, Guangzhou, Chongqing, and many other cities. I smiled, recollecting my visit back in 2007 to small (from China's perspective) cities with 2-3 million inhabitants. There I had witnessed portable traffic lights being installed at crossings and ignored by drivers. But visiting the same cities in 2017, I saw them as incarnations of Hong Kong, with its skyscrapers, highway junctions and bridges. I compared the level of monthly salaries then and now, which increased from USD 100-150 to USD 1,000-1,500 during the previous decade.

The experiment is a success. To be honest, this is an experiment with distinctive Chinese characteristics. I ask today, who did all this stuff, who has constructed a district of skyscrapers, an industrial zone or a business centre over the past 10 years. In reply, I hear different names of local Chinese officials. I ask: "Where is this official now? Has he been promoted and transferred to another province, to Beijing?" And sometimes I get an unexpected but increasingly frequent answer: "No, he is in jail". The experiment has allowed a decoding of China's economy, but has also punished the experimentalists.

The China-Belarus Industrial Park 'Great Stone' (hereinafter referred to as the Industrial Park) may become a Belarusian Hong Kong. Provided that a favourable investment environment is created, investors are enticed, site improvements are carried out, and the wellbeing of the population is improved, the Industrial Park should set an example for other Belarusian cities and an experimental site for the subsequent decoding of Belarus' entire economy.

The idea of the China-Belarus Industrial Park was put forward following the visit of Xi Jinping, in his capacity as Vice-President of the People's Republic of China, to Belarus in March 2010. In September 2011, the Government of the Republic of Belarus and the Government of the People's Republic of China signed an agreement on the development of the China-Belarus Industrial Park. Decree No. 253 "On China-Belarus Industrial Park" was issued in June 2012, and amended in May 2017 by Decree No. 166.

The Industrial Park was originally established in Belarus within the framework of China's general policy of setting up its industrial parks in foreign countries. Since 2006, China has launched active efforts to establish industrial parks in Angola, Pakistan, Thailand, Venezuela, Vietnam, Cambodia, South Korea, Egypt, Zambia, Nigeria, Mauritius, and Ethiopia. Following the establishment of the ASEAN-China Free Trade Area in 2010, the plans for the construction of joint industrial parks in every ASEAN member state were made public. Despite the general policy, there was no uniform mechanism for the establishment of those parks. They varied in size, investment arrangements, specialisation, and level and type of government support. And yet, during his state visit to Belarus in May 2015, President of China Xi Jinping called the China-Belarus Industrial Park "the Pearl on the Silk Road", thereby singling it out from the field of China's industrial parks and linking it to a different overseas strategy of China. Furthermore, it is remarkable that, as noted above, the idea of establishing the Industrial Park emerged in 2010, while the "One Belt, One Road" initiative followed in 2013. The Industrial Park has become a major project of Belarus-China cooperation and was presented at the international forum "Belt & Road" held in May 2017.

Initially, the case of the China-Singapore Industrial Park in Suzhou was used as a model by the China-Belarus Industrial Park. The former was started in China in 1992 as a follow-up to the meeting of Deng Xiaoping with Lee Kuan Yew. The leader of Singapore stressed that it had been very difficult for the Chinese officials to adopt the best Singaporean practices during their regular business trips abroad. In this regard, Singapore, together with China, would establish an industrial park, and transfer its managerial skills in the process of its development and operation. The intergovernmental agreement on the establishment of the China-Singapore Industrial Park was signed in 1994.

This park has gone through challenging establishment and development stages, including overcoming the distrust of the population, the creation of parallel parks, negative earnings, and all the rest of it. For instance, the losses faced by the joint venture managing the China-Singapore Industrial Park in its early years led to a situation where the Singapore side started selling its shares and exiting the project. Today this industrial park is one of the most successful in China. Its membership includes nearly a hundred Fortune-500 international corporations.

The secret of its success is the application of the 'one-stop shop' principle (quick resident registration), tax incentives for producers of innovative products, manufacturers of integrated circuits and software, and small businesses. The experience of the Suzhou Industrial Park in the sphere of tax incentives provided an example for the 'Great Stone' (reflected in the Decree of 2012). The tax benefits have been significantly expanded to the '10+10' format: 10 years tax-free, and half the tax rate for the next 10 years. In addition, the Decree of 2017 covered the 'one-stop shop' principle by analogy with the China-Singapore Industrial Park. However, the Suzhou experience has not been fully adapted in Belarus. It is one thing to set up a foreign industrial park in China, while it is a whole different story doing it overseas. Furthermore, this is not the 1990s anymore, and China is not Singapore, and Belarus is not China. In this regard, the industrial parks set up by China overseas are still of great practical interest.

The fundamental issue for the success of the 'Great Stone' is who acts as the main contributor of managerial skills, technologies, and international values, that are to be fostered in the Belarusian staff of the Industrial Park. At this point, certain difficulties were experienced. Initially, the major shareholder (60%) of the administration company representing the Chinese side was CAMCE, sponsored by its parent corporation, SINOMACH. However, CAMCE is an engineering company and has a vested interest in Belarus, in the form of a contracting project at Svetlogorskiy Pulp and Paper Integrated Works, and no expertise in setting up industrial parks.

In 2014, the shareholding structure of the Chinese side was changed following the visit of the Vice-Prime Minister of China, Zhang Gaoli, to Belarus. The share of CAMCE was reduced to 45.7%, and one new shareholder, China Merchants Group, entered the venture with a 20% share. This is a trade and logistics company, which has experience in setting up not industrial, but logistics parks. For this reason, the Industrial Park 'Great Stone' is still not an experimental site for decoding Belarus' economy, since there are no companies able to share the relevant values and competencies. CAMCE can share its experience in engineering and site construction, while China Merchants Group can share its sales experience. But neither has any experience in creating new industries or attracting high-tech industrial companies. It is therefore advisable to effect further changes in the shareholding structure to introduce an industry-minded company.

The Industrial Park's key focus on the high-tech industry is reflected in the fact that it was established in Belarus just for this purpose, namely, to bring in high-technology industries. Several studies conducted in Belarus show that China has surpassed Belarus by many innovation indicators.[147] This gives reason to hope for an inflow of Chinese technological investments to the Industrial Park. At the same time, it depends on Belarus' industrial needs rather than on China's technological capabilities. In this regard, the Industrial Park, with respect to the tax benefits granted for a period of twenty years, and its legal regime extending to a period of fifty years, must be an element of Belarus' industrial strategy for no less than a twenty-year period. Meanwhile, such a strategy, capable of fostering new growth areas, is hardly in evidence, and the emphasis is rather on preserving the existing production facilities. An industrial strategy requires, in the first place, an audit of the industrial complex to assess long-term competitive advantages and disadvantages, consequences of WTO membership, etc. The Ministry of Industrial Policy, created by merging several ministries and concerns, may form the institutional framework for Belarusian industrialisation by means of the transition to public administration of the entire industry, rather than individual state-owned enterprises. Thus, it is the development of an industrial strategy that will allow the Industrial Park to become a mechanism for implementing structural reforms in the Belarusian economy, the starting point being its industry.

The industrial strategy involves the determination of new technological growth areas of the Belarusian economy. The Regulations on the China-Belarus Industrial Park, approved by the Resolution of the Council of Ministers of the Republic of Belarus, No. 756, dated 16 August 2012, specify the following priority activities of the Industrial Park: electronics, fine chemicals, biotechnology, engineering, and advanced materials. Still, according to some sources, the nature of the new world industry in the next ten years will be determined by such sectors as robotics, genetics, and big data processing, accompanied by the codification of money and markets.[148,149,150] CEOs of transnational corporations in China, the US, and the EU, forecast the development of such sectors as data processing systems, the Internet of Things, etc. (Table 9).

Table 9: Ranking of the future importance of industries, based on a survey of CEOs of transnational corporations.[151]

	China	USA	EU
Data processing and forecasting systems	1	1	4
Smart factories (Internet of Things)	2	4	1
High-performance computing	3	6	7
Advanced materials	4	3	5
Interaction design	5	5	3
Augmented reality (to improve quality, training, expert knowledge)	6	10	8
Smart products (Internet of Things)	7	2	2
Robotics	8	7	6
Open-source software (direct customer input)	10	9	10
3D technologies	11	8	9

The new Decree of 2017 does not specify, but rather eases, technological requirements for accession to the Industrial Park. However, this is not a fundamental concern. In any case, in order to ensure its innovativeness, the Industrial Park would focus more specifically not on implementation of domestic technologies, but on the transfer of advanced foreign ones. This would call for an appropriate infrastructure for their transfer, development, and commercialisation. Moreover, the ultimate goal of the Industrial Park should be the creation of an environment favourable for home-grown innovations and the emergence of competitive domestic technologies.

Alongside the hope that China would focus its high-tech investments on Belarus, there are arguments to the contrary. Firstly, in recent years, there has been an outflow of productive assets from China to nearby countries (for instance, Vietnam, Bangladesh) that demonstrate a better balance of costs and productivity than China (and Belarus). This is especially the case for the labour force. Secondly, Western companies that came to China in the 1990s and 2000s are currently going back to developed countries. This is due to the development of robotics there, when the price of robots declines over time as their performance improves (in accordance with Moore's law). To remain competitive, China also prioritises robotics: the annual growth of this sector in China in recent years has been 25%.[152] In view of the foregoing, China's priority may shift in the long run, from offshore manufacturing towards the retention of companies inside the country in order to maintain jobs and social stability. In this regard, China and Belarus are actually competitors for technology, while the Industrial Park serves as a means of attracting primarily international, rather than just Chinese, technological investments.

Russian Kaluga oblast, with one million inhabitants, could be an example of foreign direct investment mobilisation for the Industrial Park. Its governor has succeeded in attracting over USD 1 billion owing to its industrial parks. Another example is the Suzhou Industrial Park, with an index of 'investment density' of over USD 1.7 billion per square kilometre. At the same time, care should be taken to distinguish between investments for the establishment of a park and investments into an already established park:

a) *investments in the establishment of the Industrial Park*. According to the Ministry of Economy, investments needed over the next 10-15 years to develop the infrastructure of the 'Great Stone' are estimated at USD 5-6 billion. Nevertheless, the expected size of Chinese investments into the Industrial Park's infrastructure might prove to be overoptimistic. First of all, in many foreign industrial parks and Belarusian free trade zones, the infrastructure, together with 'amenities' options, is provided by the state, free of charge. Therefore, major foreign investments flow into already operating industrial parks rather than into those being established. Secondly, China's *de facto* investments into overseas industrial parks under construction are normally lower than planned (Table 10).

Table 10: Estimated and actual foreign direct investment from China in selected overseas industrial parks[153]

Chinese industrial park, host country	Construction start date	Area size, ha	Estimated construction investments, million USD	Actual construction investment, million USD
TEDA, Egypt	2000	134	200 – 280	49
Chambishi, Zambia	2004	1158	200	150
Lekki, Nigeria	2007	109	392	83
Jinfei, Mauritius	2009	70	220	15
Ogun, Nigeria	2009	250	220	24
Eastern, Ethiopia	2010	200	101	22

b) *investments into the established Industrial Park*. To make the high technologies employed cost effective, high-technology enterprises normally focus on large-scale production and broad markets. These include the developed markets of the US and the EU, as well as the growing market of China, rather than the import-substituting market of the Russian Federation, subject to the sanctions. In this regard, the Industrial Park's export orientation towards the Eurasian market alone is insufficient to generate an inflow of high-tech direct investments.

The formation of a new business environment in the Industrial Park involves the creation of new jobs. The number of employees per square kilometre at foreign industrial parks depends upon the type of technology, the number of inhabitants in adjacent settlements, and the infrastructure. For instance, the number of employees per square kilometre at the Chinese Industrial Park 'E-Town', located near Beijing, is 14.9 thousand people, at WaiGaoQian, near Shanghai it is 19 thousand people, at the park in Suzhou it is 2.8 thousand people, and at the French park, Sophia Antipolis, it is 1.3 thousand people. In terms of the French 'benchmark', the number of employees at the 'Great Stone', which covers 91.5 square kilometres, may total 120 thousand people. At the same time, the Industrial Park is about creating highly skilled jobs. As an illustration, this can be achieved if a single chain of scientific, manufacturing, and commercial organisations is formed, beginning with start-ups. Only skilled professionals can generate high added value. In that respect, the Industrial Park must become attractive not only to highly skilled Belarusians, but also to foreign specialists, including not merely seasonal workers but also engineers, architects, scientists, and businessmen. This requires not only manufacturing facilities, but also a modern social, cultural, and residential infrastructure. This lays the groundwork for high performance, a comfortable life, and personal fulfilment for young, creative, and resourceful people. For instance, the comfortable social infrastructure is precisely the reason why many highly-skilled IT specialists choose to reside in Singapore and American cities.

Apart from the social infrastructure, an important incentive to draw residents to the Industrial Park is tax benefits. To be sure, the incentives offered at the 'Great Stone' are more attractive than at other industrial parks, particularly with regard to the profit tax (Table 11).

Table 11: Profit tax benefits for technological park residents across the world[154]

<table>
<tr><th>Industrial park</th><th colspan="2">Profit tax</th></tr>
<tr><td>China-Belarus Industrial Park (Belarus)</td><td colspan="2">'10+10' – residents of the Industrial Park are exempted from profit tax for 10 years following the date of reporting profits, and pay half the profit tax rate for 10 subsequent years</td></tr>
<tr><td rowspan="3">China Industrial Park in Ho Chi Minh City (Vietnam)</td><td rowspan="3">Initial stage (1995-2009)</td><td>'4+4' – residents of the park exporting over 80% of the manufactured goods are exempted from profit tax for 4 years following the date of reporting profits, and pay half the profit tax rate for 4 subsequent years.</td></tr>
<tr><td>'2+3' – residents of the park exporting 50% to 80% of the manufactured goods are exempted from profit tax for 2 years following the date of reporting profits, and pay half the profit tax rate for 3 subsequent years.</td></tr>
<tr><td>'1+2' – residents of the park exporting up to 50% of the manufactured goods are exempted from profit tax for 1 year following the date of reporting profits, and pay half the profit tax rate for 2 subsequent years</td></tr>
</table>

Industrial park	Profit tax	
	Current stage (2010 – present)	'2+4' – residents of the park are exempted from profit tax for 2 years following the date of reporting profits, and pay half the profit tax rate for 4 subsequent years.
China-Singapore Industrial Park in Suzhou (China)	Initial stage (1995-2007)	'2+3' – residents registered for a period of 10 or more years benefit from a profit tax exemption for two years following the date of reporting profits, and pay 50% of the general tax rate for 3 subsequent years.
	Current stage (2008 – present)	Residents of the Industrial Park involved in the innovation sector pay profit tax at the rate of 10%. The basic profit tax rate in China is 25%.
St. Petersburg Special Economic Zone (Russia)	Residents pay profit tax at the rate of 15.5%. The basic profit tax rate in Russia is 20%.	

Another incentive that attracts residents to industrial parks is the quality and cost of the offered infrastructure services. The internal infrastructure includes a package of so called '9 amenities': electricity, water, sewerage, paved roads, gas, telecommunications, heating, mail, and television, as well as land levelling and setting up production facilities. This will reduce the start-up costs of resident investors of the Park. The cost of modern infrastructure for a technological park is continuously increasing. For instance, 20 years ago, the average cost of one square kilometre of internal infrastructure of an industrial park in China was CNY 200 million (USD 23 million), while at present, that average indicator is up to CNY 500 million (around USD 80 million). The cost of one square kilometre for residents of the 'Great Stone' is approximately USD 45. By comparison, it constitutes USD 15 for residents of the China-Vietnam Industrial Park in Ho Chi Minh City. Park residents' costs also include the wages and salaries of employees. For instance, the average salary in Belarus was USD 300-400 in 2017, while at the China-Vietnam Industrial Park it was USD 250 for employees and USD 1,000 for managerial staff.

The 'Great Stone' has seemingly obvious advantages in the form of tax privileges, low labour costs, and infrastructure. Thus, a massive inflow of residents into the Industrial Park should be expected, provided that large-scale presentations and forums are held. However, this is not the case. In 2016, although more than 100 presentations were made, and over 300 people representing 150 companies visited the Industrial Park, only one resident was registered at the Industrial Park in 2016! Later from 2016 to 2019 the number of the residents has increased.

The analogy between the 'Great Stone' and the construction of the new high-tech hub of Xiongan in China, announced on 1 April 2017, is even more confusing. This hub will coordinate the development of Beijing, Tianjin, and Hebei, and, according to expert views, will become a new Shenzhen. The most remarkable feature of this story, however, is the reaction of companies and common people, who believed in this project and decided to contribute their own money. In addition to a sharp increase in quotations for construction, real estate, and industrial companies, there is feverish demand for residential property in the counties adjacent to Xiongan. The situation has become so serious that the issue has urgently been put on the agenda of the State Council, which cancelled and suspended all deals closed after 1 April 2017 and established on-going monitoring of the situation in the whole region. The case of Xiongan, contrasted with the 'Great Stone', is disturbing. While China is trying to prevent excessive commotion among investors, Belarus endeavours to introduce a spirit of optimism in them. That means there is something else that influences investors' mood – the prospect of markets for products.

The main constraining factors, which hinder the recruitment of high-tech Chinese companies as residents of the 'Great Stone' Industrial Park, include the low capacity of the Belarusian market, the volatility of the Russian market, and the closeness of the European market. In its turn, the rapidly growing and increasingly more expensive market of China is more attractive for EU and US companies as it employs more advanced technologies, compared to the PRC. However, these companies are not always ready to establish production facilities there, fearing the transfer of their technologies to China. In this regard, in order to ensure the arrival of international companies with the most advanced technologies, it is advisable to offer them duty-free access to China's market, i.e. to set up a free-trade area between the Industrial Park and China. This, in turn, will ensure a duty-free inflow of Chinese components and improve the competitiveness of production. The next step could be to set up a similar free-trade area between the Industrial Park and the EU. It is obvious that this proposal is not aligned with the existing legislation of either Belarus or the EAEU. Nevertheless, it could become the experimental site to ensure commercial cooperation between the EAEU and China.

A similar idea of establishing a small EU-China free-trade area is being implemented by Georgia. In May 2017, an agreement on the establishment of a free-trade area was signed by China and Georgia in Beijing. In view of the existing EU-Georgia preferential trade regime, Georgia is expected to become a key regional platform for EU-oriented Chinese direct investment, as well as China-oriented European investment starting from 2018. It may also significantly re-target the 'One Belt, One Road' trajectory in the post-soviet region, and reduce the relative attractiveness of the 'Great Stone'.

Removing barriers to investors coming to the 'Great Stone' does not address the country-specific challenges that led to investment reversal in Belarus. It is therefore important for the Industrial Park to overcome the deficiencies of the country's investment climate. The matters of principle are:

a) guaranteed property rights, especially intellectual property rights, through the application, for instance, of British law on the territory of the Industrial Park;
b) easy business registration, operation, and exit, based on the principle of 'one stop shop' represented by the administration of the Industrial Park.[155]

These tasks essentially entail establishing two jurisdictions within one territory, as exampled by Hong Kong-China ('one country – two systems'), the project of the Astana Financial Centre in Kazakhstan, the Dubai Financial Centre in the UAE, and the project of Lazika city in Georgia.[156] Nothing other than the fundamental alienation of the Industrial Park activity from the Belarusian national investment climate, while preserving its territorial affiliation and economic immunity, will make 'greenfield' investments more attractive to elite transnational corporations with new technologies, which could then be followed by a massive inflow of world business.

Therefore, the inflow of foreign investment to the 'Great Stone' is discouraged, particularly by investors who fear investing in Belarus. Thus, on one hand, for the Industrial Park to be fully operational the Belarusian legal regime that influences the investment climate needs to be changed significantly, while, on the other hand, if the investment climate is sufficiently modified, this would mean decoding the entire Belarusian economy, and, hence, the Industrial Park itself would no longer be needed.

CHAPTER 8

"BECAUSE WE DECIDED SO"

After Belarus' economy is decoded, "because I decided so" will be replaced with "because we decided so." It will be replaced, rather than developing into, 'we', from a plethora of 'I's'. The very decision, 'so', comes to the forefront, now being clear and obvious not only to the person, who makes it, but to all those around. And then it is a collective decision, which reflects the interests of many individuals united by a common goal, a common 'we'. The main thing decoding changes is the atmosphere of decision-making. In this regard, while earlier, in the context of "because I decided so", all decisions seemed wrong, untimely, and ineffective, now, in the context of "because we decided so", the same decisions would seem correct, essential, and useful. The solution is that now any individual 'I' has a counterweight in the form of a public (not sovereign) 'we'. Now, these 'I' and 'we' share both the responsibility and the authority, they complement and restrain each other. But to achieve this, 'we' must grow stronger, gain weight, and self-identify. And here the main question arises: Who are we? Who will Belarusians be akin to? What new features will they develop after decoding, and how will those affect the economy?

Certainty

Certainty is the opposite of doublethink. It instils the clarity of thinking, confidence, and calm behaviour. Certainty calls for sincerity, social unity, a consolidation of broken thinking, and collective memory. That could be achieved only through social dialogue, finding some common views of the past, the present, and the future. The decoding of Belarus' economy raises major issues and requires certainty, a clear choice and clear answers to key questions. Capitalism or communism? Market or administrative tools? Europe or Russia?

Capitalism or Communism?

Social evolution has proved that the option of the market economy is the only possible basis for the development of mankind. At each stage of its development, the market economy acquired new forms, progressing from simple commodity production to more advanced arrangements. In the period of slavery and feudalism, there was simple commodity production, when goods were exchanged by means of money. Labour relations were mainly based on exploitation, and workers (slaves, serfs) were not free, unlike their employers. Capitalism has introduced such elements as private ownership, competition, a stronger influence of supply and demand on economic processes, improved efficiency of capital management, capital spill-overs from one sphere to another, liberation of labour in choosing its sphere of application, optimal allocation of labour, goods, and information. Exploitation was replaced with partnerships established on a contractual basis, with increasing compensation for labour and employees getting more and more freedom. That has led to the birth of a classical market economy. At the present stage of capitalist development, the state reinforces its role by constantly increasing deductions from the added value, to finance social government programmes. This gives the market economy the status of a social economy.

In the framework of a market economy, such obvious advantages of capitalism as dynamism, fast implementation of innovations, and improvement of wellbeing, are combined with the orientation of the society towards maximising profits that sometimes overrides other values. This creates a consumer society, in which income growth provokes higher spending, which, in turn, leads to the irrational use of raw materials, and a growing gap between countries and between individuals. In pursuit of high, and sometimes unlimited, incomes, one can become a workaholic, wasting health and life. As an illustration, some employees of the Chinese corporation, Huawei, died while in their office workplaces, being incentivised to earn money, get huge bonuses and shares of their company, which were continuously growing in value. It should be stressed, however, that such orientation and consumer behaviour in the context of market relations is voluntary. An individual always has the right to make his own choice between self-sacrifice at work, to meet his growing needs, pushed by advertising, fashion, social status, public opinion, and other factors, or a moderate, decent standard of living, combined with a rich cultural and social life.

Communism has become the alternative and the antithesis of capitalism. Its ideas have turned into a kind of religion because of the prevalence of faith over the understanding of the realities of human needs and psychology. Attempts to achieve communist ideals led to the creation of socialism, which developed into Bolshevism as an extreme, anti-humane, form of establishing social equality.[157] The methods of implementing this idea included the total control and regulation of all aspects of human life, which practically deadlocked the development of the society. The main thing was the embodiment of the invented and theorised ideas of communism which turned a man into a cog in the state machine, into state property. In practice, it resulted in a sharp restriction of man's pursuance of freedom, initiative, and creative work, as he was programmed to address the tasks set by the state and often unrelated to his interests. The after-effects of that system are still faced by many post-Soviet countries, including Belarus. With some elements of a market economy and democracy emerging in these countries, their people were unprepared to accept the freedom that the market economy offers and responded with doublethink and orientation towards the Soviet past. But being constantly in a borderline state, balancing between communism and capitalism, is an illusion. In any case, with the orientation to the Soviet past, socialist elements are regenerated in the economy in a natural way, which leads to a slide into socialism and, eventually, to communism. Therefore, it is important to remember that the choice of capitalism is inevitable for a society that declares wellbeing and development as its priority.

Market or Administrative Tools?

The choice of capitalism rather than communism encourages the use of market, rather than administrative, tools. But in practice, this does not always work. Many countries that operate within the framework of capitalism and market relations tend to use administrative, repressive, measures. According to the 2016 index of economic freedom, half of the world's 180 countries (92 countries) are considered moderately free, mostly free, or free market economies. The other half (88 countries) are mostly unfree and repressed.[158] The latter group of countries, with, as a rule, underdeveloped economies, tries unsuccessfully to become economically developed through non-market methods. They are doomed to be constantly catching up, because in the absence of a market and the predominant reliance on repressive tools, an economy would be able to achieve only a certain level of development, becoming moderately developed at best. Then the economy either gets stuck at this level or goes into recession (the 'middle income' trap).

Absolutely all developed countries have a free market economy. Therefore, their further development is influenced by other factors, rather than the choice between administrative and market instruments of economic regulation. The correlation between the level of economic freedom of 180 countries and the GDP per capita, is 0.596 for 2016.[159] The greatest interdependence is registered in countries with a moderate level of economic development and a moderate level of economic freedom. This suggests that market instruments have the greatest effect on stimulating the economy precisely at the moderate level of its development. In other words, only market (structural) transformation would enable further development and a departure from the middle group.

In Belarus, the understanding of the irreversibility of the market economy and its acceptance by society would create certainty. The Belarusian society would then develop its market-oriented thinking and appropriate attitudes and behaviour, such as autonomy, responsibility, independence, and an orientation to minimising costs and maximising profits. This would change the financial mentality of Belarusians, shifting the focus from consumption and saving to investment. In this regard, the Belarusian society would face competitive tension that is essential to stimulate the economy. Next, social demand would be generated for all elements of the classical market economy – privatisation, the rule of law, entrepreneurship, free movement of financial and labour resources, orderly strategic planning, etc. In response to the social demand, the state management of the economy would also gain certainty, as its absence preserves doublethink and conservatism. When the certainty is established, all the internal energy that is burned off within doublethink would be directed outward, to support the work of creative mechanisms and develop innovative solutions. Under the changed conditions, it would become obvious which government bodies are needed, what their functions should be, and what role the state should play in the economy. The attitude of the society and government bodies to businesses would be simplified. It would be universally understood that an enterprise of any form of ownership is created with just one goal – to maximise profits. Any other tasks related to social functions, national security, etc. are within the competence of the state, while for businesses, they serve only as tools to gain profits. The certainty emerging in Belarus would become more understandable and attractive for others, and for foreign investors. This would create prerequisites for economic stability, long-term planning, and investments.

Certainty of the social orientation to capitalism and market instruments would transform the national features, eliminating doublethink, the orientation towards the Soviet past and paternalism, replacing them with other, less complicated and more understandable, characteristics. The unexpected charisma would also give way to predictable professionalism, which stimulates the economy.

Europe or Russia?

Certainty over the choice between capitalism and communism, between market and administrative tools, leads to certainty over the choice between Europe and Russia. If the society is oriented to the market economy, it becomes easier to answer the question of which cultural matrix is closer to Belarus – the European or the Russian.

In the environment of economic pragmatism, it becomes obvious that there can be no economic choice between the European and the Russian cultural matrices for Belarusians. When the Belarusian cultural matrix is decoded, a different kind of logic, a different frame of reference and cultural values, first and foremost economic, would be established. If it is beneficial to cooperate with both Europe and Russia, there is no need to choose. The platform of common benefits could bring together the European matrix and the Russian one. The geographical determinism pushes Belarus to play the role of a platform for interweaving European and Russian economic interests, their joint business. Therefore, the issue is not the choice between Europe and Russia, but the combination of their interests and values in Belarus. This involves building relations with each of the parties that would be mutually beneficial and not to the detriment of the other party.

In today's environment, with the confrontation between Russia and the West (Europe, the USA), Belarus' certainty over economic cooperation with all the parties seems utopian and too rational. At the same time, rational reasoning with a priority focus on the national interest is useful here. On the one hand, one cannot fail to notice that Russia tends to reunite the post-Soviet area, preventing its neighbouring countries from leaving for the sphere of influence of the EU, Turkey, and China. On the other hand, it is obvious that the geopolitical and economic situation of Belarus calls for developing relations with all its partners instead of becoming isolated and focusing on just one. In this regard, Belarus has nothing to do but insist on being respected, defend its independence, and seek new forms of cooperation with neighbouring countries. The experience of Georgia and Ukraine proves that it is possible. But, their experience points out the risk of paying the high price of losing human lives and part of the territory. To prevent this, it is necessary to decode the matrices of neighbouring countries, overcome the military mentality, insist on respecting Belarus' interests, and acknowledge that Belarus follows universal international values. The latter could become the link between the European and Russian cultural matrices in Belarus. If one of the sides ignores universal human values, infringes on Belarus' sovereignty and territorial integrity, there would be nothing left but to take sides and choose one partner for cooperation, including economic cooperation.

In the absence of a peaceful coexistence between Europe and Russia, the fate of Belarus is worrying. It makes Belarus place its national interests above the geopolitical interests of its neighbouring countries. In this case, there is an understanding that Belarus is a small country that belongs to itself, not to one of the matrices, and should not be involved in a conflict between large countries and regions. Belarusians would realise that they cannot have any 'big brother', no one owes them anything, and that no one would help them, except themselves. Such a syndrome of isolation, a sense of belonging to a small country, and striving to be self-sufficient in the face of a shortage of human and natural resources, is the very sense of independence. All these elements seem to form an insurmountable cultural flaw. But, judging by the experience of Singapore, Israel, and a number of other countries, this flaw can be turned into an advantage by changing the attitude of the society towards it. Furthermore, this advantage can be persistently developed by cultivating national pride, independence, and responsibility, on the basis of the new decoded features. This would relieve the feeling of paternalism, orientation towards the Soviet past, and orientation to scale, and create conditions for the restructuring and diversification of the economy. This could be accompanied by a phobia of defencelessness, and the emergence of the 'fear of all', that is illustrated by Switzerland, Singapore, and Israel. At the same time, economic rationalism and openness must prevail over fear and isolation, which would make Belarus a platform for the arrival of interweaving universal world values.

Courage

Courage is nurtured by certainty. If it is clear what should be defended, what values and positions should be supported, then there is courage, bravery, and fidelity to principles. However, it should be noted that economic certainty is not enough for courage. Society should also accept other universal values, such as decency, dignity, honesty, humanity, frugality, orientation to the future, education, success, ethics, mutual respect, and trust. It is primarily faith and self-confidence that nurture courage and defeat fear. Overcoming fear eliminates the orientation towards the Soviet past and paternalism. This removes the impending doom of living a complete lie, walking around in circles, and repeating past mistakes. It opens up an opportunity for experiments, innovations, and entrepreneurship, which boosts economic growth. Courage becomes synonymous with accelerated progress. At the same time, the feeling of courage injects 'cultural adrenaline', which forms the need for speed, the rebellious spirit, and even a certain addiction to courageous actions. But it is important to keep the balance, to stay in this state while growing bold. On the one hand, not to return to the arbitrariness and irrationality of the familiar "because I decided so". On the other hand, not to go to the other extreme and succumb to the market-induced feelings of greed and selfishness. It is essential to feel the limit of courage, the fine line of public interest. Courage should become a striking feature of Belarusians, displayed at the right time, rather than a permanent state of imbalance and unpredictability.

Certainty and courage help support economic rationalism. As an illustration, bold decisions are made to minimise cultural barriers if the social focus shifts to the economy. An example of such a decision could be the rational choice of the language of the fastest growing, promising, and popular market, as a means of communication within the framework of the domestic economy. Given the current level of development of different economies, the rate of their economic growth, and their population size, English and Chinese appear to be the priority languages for attracting investment (Table 12). In turn, the use of the Russian language in the economy (similar to Portuguese in the world economy), and especially the Belarusian one, is a cultural barrier to business. But this does not mean avoiding these languages. The economy can equally quench or revive interest in a language. For example, in the middle of the 20th century, few could have guessed that the Chinese language would now be in demand. Just as in the 15th to 19th centuries, Spanish, which today cannot be attributed to the most popular group, was the language of the world economy. With the economic recovery in Russia and Belarus and the deepening of their markets, the interest in their languages will also be revived. For the time being, national languages serve as cultural symbols and, in the context of decoding the economy, call for bold rational solutions.

Table 12: Countries by level of economic development, population size, and languages used[160]

Country	GDP (real), 2015, USD trillion	Real economic growth, 2015, in %	Population size, million people	National language
USA	18.0	2.6	324.5	English
EU	16.2	1.8	510.1	Multiple languages
China	11.0	6.9	1,381.6	Chinese
Japan	4.1	0.6	126.8	Japanese
India	2.1	7.3	1,312.1	English, Hindi
Brazil	1.7	-3.8	207.1	Portuguese
Russia	1.3	-3.7	146.8	Russian
Mexico	1.1	2.3	122.2	Spanish
Indonesia	0.8	4.7	260.6	English, Indonesian slang
Nigeria	0.4	4.0	186.9	English
Philippines	0.3	5.9	103.6	English, Filipino
Pakistan	0.2	4.2	196.4	English, Urdu

Openness

Courage nurtures openness. Fear prevents openness, and leads to isolation and becoming enclosed within one's cultural matrix. Initially, openness can cause discomfort and is painful. But ultimately, through the formation of a constantly updated information environment, openness leads to a change and development of the way of life - destiny. Socially 'archived' information is decoded only with openness and communication, by coming into contact with people representing a different culture. As in psychotherapy, social diseases can be cured only through openness and a frank public dialogue.

Openness is faced with a dilemma. On the one hand, the society may need to set a limit to decoding that would prevent its depersonalisation, loss of cultural identity and national values. Openness, as well as, say, publicity, has a limit, which is one's right to privacy. If the society has a strong sense of national pride, bleeding historical wounds, then it is entitled to establish its own limit to decoding. In this case, the national identity will be combined with the pride of its openness and cooperation with advanced world practices. On the other hand, one should always realise that any limit is a barrier to initiative, growth, and development of the economy. In addition, the society is prone to make mistakes. The public may be unaware of how understated or inflated their expectations are and how far the limit could be pushed. Therefore, it is precisely overcoming the barriers of public expectations that helps achieve progress in development. Openness makes it possible to adopt the best and most effective world practices, and improve them within the local environment.

Openness of the economy starts with trade. The trade channel provides an opportunity to use a number of economic tools to boost economic growth, such as depreciation (to push exports, reduce government spending, decrease the real incomes of the population) to contain imports.[161] But openness, working only through the trade channel, cannot generate sound results. No high correlation between the trade openness of the economy (exports and imports to GDP) and GDP per capita has been discovered. The evidence of 150 countries for 2015-2016 gives a correlation coefficient of 0.407.

Openness also enables engagement with the financial channel. As soon as a country opens up, it instils optimism among investors, attracting them into the country, resulting in its economic growth based on their expectations. At the same time, due to information asymmetry, investors may not always be sufficiently well-informed and thus tend to copy each other, following the 'herd' instinct. Investors are guided by the rankings of international rating agencies, the media, insider information, rumours, associative analogies with similar markets, industries, and financial instruments, and thus, their expectations may not always be sufficiently substantiated.[162] If such expectations change and investors become disappointed, say, in the authorities' commitment to maintaining the policies of openness, a reversal of investments may occur. This is rather difficult, and it takes a long time to restore credibility with investors and creditors. It often calls for rebooting the management system in the economy, reshuffling senior officials, demonstrating in practice that the economic authorities are taking real steps. For instance, many countries adopt economic programmes, including specific public steps, the implementation of which, in a timely manner, is transparent and compelling for the society and investors. As an illustration, in 2015, Kazakhstan announced the Plan of the Nation; 100 specific steps to implement five institutional reforms. Similar reforms have been announced in recent years in Bangladesh, Myanmar, and Uzbekistan. The verifiable consistency and efficiency of the economic authorities help gain credibility with the international community, which is essential for long-term investment and sustainable economic growth.

The openness of the economy implies competition and adaptability. The fear of losing out through competition leads to half-openness, the search for weak competitors, and to non-competitive markets. Only complete openness, which has internalised the spirit of competition, can make the economy stronger and contribute to practical learning. Courage generates the acceptance of the fact that losing a competition is a lesson to be learnt, an opportunity for adaptation. Adaptability involves the perception of a different cultural matrix, not through the demonstration of one's superiority over a competitor, and not through his humiliation, but through adopting his best qualities and imitating his strengths. Imitation is often a source of innovation. The national matrix gets stronger in the context of constant openness, competition and adaptation. It becomes more attractive for others, which appeals to strong counterparts, and further improves competition and adaptation. Openness always offers options, alternatives, different examples that form a vision of the future, and a development path based on best practices. All this would downplay such Belarusian features as orientation to the past and paternalism.

Tolerance

Tolerance arises from openness. One can check the level of his tolerance only in real life, in practice. Tactlessness and discrimination emerge only when there are objects or subjects of potential discrimination – people of a different sex, race, faith, shape, colour, sexual orientation, etc. Test your level of tolerance by leafing through the French satirical magazine *Charlie Hebdo*, or by being face-to-face with a person of a different cultural matrix. Until this happens, one maintains the self-soothing illusion of his tolerance. In his speech at TEDx, former UN Resident Coordinator and UNDP Resident Representative, Sanaka Samarasinha, asked a rhetorical question: "In Belarus, there are more than 0.5 million, who live with different types of disabilities, … out of a population of 9.4. If you go out into the streets, you do not see them very often. Where are they?".[163] Probably at home because there is no barrier-free environment. In addition, according to the Pew Research Center, 85% of Belarusians "consider homosexuality morally unacceptable".[164] Thus, there are psychological barriers in the society, which, in fact, considers itself tolerant due to the absence of objects for discrimination.

Such self-deception about tolerance is typical of societies at different levels of development. Some hide behind their poverty and weakness, saying that they have to survive in the competitive environment, and, thus, cannot accept a compromise or be tolerant of the interests of others. Others, on the contrary, hide their unwillingness to compromise behind their strength and wealth, and say that they simply do not want to show tolerance. But these societies are mistaken in both cases. Tolerance is necessary to achieve sustainable progress and to maintain individual freedom, both in the economic and political spheres. In the absence of tolerance in the first case, wellbeing cannot be improved, while in the second case it can be quickly lost. Tolerance allows individualism to be revealed, it opens up opportunities to see the invisible, the substance hidden behind the form, the essence of any problem, and to find non-standard solutions for faster adaptation and the development of the society.

In the economy, tolerance generates the main thing – the atmosphere of trust, mutual respect, security, professional thinking and behaviour, and public orientation to long-term results. Thanks to tolerance, trust is formed from the bottom up. It does not arise from top-down orders and instructions. Therefore, tolerance and trust exclude paternalism, as well as authoritarianism and dirigisme. The atmosphere of tolerance helps the economy grow at the speed of trust; trust in each other, in society, in strangers rather than in institutions, and in law and government. This creates a comfortable environment for self-realisation, a focus on professional qualities, with no energy wasted on self-identification, self-defence or proof of one's cultural features. Wasting energy on discrimination and, therefore, on searching for errors, causes, and punishments, rather than on solving problems, prevents realisation of economic potential and constrains economic growth.

Tolerance correlates to various indicators reflecting the development of society and the economy – the GDP per capita, the index of entrepreneurship, the index of competitiveness, etc. (Table 13).

Table 13: Coefficients of tolerance (racial, ethnic, gay and lesbian) correlation to a range of indicators[165]

To the GDP per capita	0.637
To the GDP per capita (2016)	0.591
To the Global Competitiveness Index	0.564
To the Index of Entrepreneurship	0.608
To the Human Development Index	0.504
To Urbanisation	0.410
To the Inequality Index	-0.038
To the Index of Economic Freedom (2016)	0.426
To the Democracy Index (2016)	0.567

Tolerance accepts, and simultaneously calls into question, any theory, dogma, ideology, or cultural matrix, including the economic one. However, it disregards the first, often biased and erroneous impression, which appears under the influence of one's cultural matrix. In the environment of tolerance, any irrational belief, any firm ungrounded attitude to the country's economic development, any deep optimism or pessimism, become the psyche of fatalism. Tolerance develops a different cultural matrix based on reality, facts, and practical provability. All this forms an independent dogma of economic pragmatism and rationalism. Accepting different ideas based on practical experience and experiments creates the basis for the empirical advancement of the economy. This is confirmed, for example, by the experience of transnational corporations employing people of different nationalities — they are more successful since they find common ground in the form of universal values, multiculturalism, and professionalism. In Belarus, EPAM Systems is an example of such a multicultural corporation — it was the first in the region of Central and Eastern Europe to run its IPO at the New York Stock Exchange. Another confirmation is the success of multicultural Singapore and Hong Kong, China – with their economic policies of pragmatism over demagogy.

Pluralism

Pluralism arises from tolerance. It manifests itself in an atmosphere of mutual respect. According to Immanuel Kant, respect means recognising the right of others to be different. Pluralism is not just diversity of individuals, but complementarity of differences, and the generation of common energy. At the same time, in the context of diversity of opinions and values, conflicts are unavoidable. In the environment of pluralism, disputes and differences occur before a decision is taken, but then, if the decision-making mechanism is accepted, once a decision is adopted, everyone moves in the same direction. Since tolerance nurtures individualism, pluralism nurtures healthy collectivism, a collaborative collective of individualists.

Pluralism is achieved not only through declaration and persuasion. Practical mechanisms in the framework of educational paternalism are also essential when governmental and public organisations work, and the government implements specific social policies to support pluralism. This entails the equal access of different social groups to mass media, to political life, and the diversified living environment. The introduction of quotas for residents of one race, nationality, or minority living in the same house, following Singapore's example, would eliminate the problem of ghettos, and so on.[166]

Pluralism ensures economy stability. This is achieved because of the interdependence of opposing views and their general orientation to one goal – wellbeing based on the principles of the market economy (the model of 'collective liberalism'). However, such interdependence arises not through administrative subordination, but on the basis of the voluntary trust in each other and in institutions. Pluralism and collective liberalism are nurtured through a common understanding of problems, and the perception of common threats to the wellbeing of each individual, which unites autonomous individuals. Pluralism offers an opportunity to search for a variety of solutions to the most complex problems, and thereby ensures some dynamic stability of the entire economic system. In the economy, pluralism entails a balanced combination and complementarity of different forms of ownership, multiple structures of private interests, opinions and contradictions. It crystallises managerial decisions, allows minority interests to be taken into account, and builds a system of checks and balances, incentives, and automatic stabilisers. Just like tolerance, pluralism is formed from the bottom up, rather than the top down, and thus, both are incompatible with paternalism, authoritarianism, and dirigisme. Pluralism in the economy projects this feature to politics, generates social demand for a multi-party system, the development of new socio-political relations, and democratic institutions. The resulting classical democratic regime, in return, reinforces the market economy. The correlation between the level of development of democracy and the level of economic freedom, based on the evidence of 150 countries for 2016, is 0.627. There is a certain interrelationship between the levels of democracy in a country and the development of its economy (GDP per capita), with a correlation coefficient of 0.533. However, taking into account the experience of certain countries, such as the People's Republic of China and Singapore, there is no straightforward scientific evidence to prove that political democracy leads to the development of the economy.

The above features, including certainty, courage, openness, tolerance and pluralism, established after decoding, also have an effect on the economy in their own way. But this effect is differently oriented and limited. It is oriented to ensuring the wellbeing of the population based on universal human values and the principles of a market economy. It is limited by social certainty and the collective courage to defend this certainty. At the same time, such features as openness, tolerance, and pluralism, facilitate unimpeded transmittance of economic impulses, which reduces the importance of the cultural matrix, making the economic matrix a priority. Therefore, within the new decoded cultural matrix, it is increasingly difficult to trace its impact on the economy. And, thus, within the new matrix, the topic under analysis yields its relevance to something else, which influences economic decisions and behaviour more than the matrix. As a result, the behavioural economics of Belarus would turn classical.

At the end of this chapter, I would still like to visualise the matrix that would be formed after decoding the Belarusian economy, to see who the Belarusians would resemble. At present, there are countries and regions in the world that, in one way or another, combine all the above features. Examples include the following ten countries (Table 14).

Table 14: Ten benchmarks for Belarus' economy following its decoding[167][168][169]

Index	Switzerland	Australia	Denmark	Holland	Canada	New Zealand	Sweden	Ireland	Singapore	Hong Kong
Index of Economic Freedom, country ranking, 2017	4	5	19	16	7	3	20	9	2	1
Tolerance index, country ranking, 2015	17	4	13	6	1	3	10	7	23	30
Democracy Index, country ranking, 2016	7	6	4	10	8	5	2	13	81	63
GDP per capita, country ranking, 2016	2	10	8	13	16	21	11	4	9	14
Global Competitiveness Index, country ranking, 2017	1	22	12	4	15	13	6	23	2	9
Human Development Index, country ranking, 2016	2	2	5	7	10	13	14	8	5	12
Happy Planet Index, country ranking, 2016	2	9	1	7	6	8	10	19	22	75
Overall index (based on summing up the rankings)	1 (35)	2 (58)	3 (62)	4 (63)	4 (63)	5 (66)	6 (73)	7 (83)	8 (144)	9 (204)

Looking at the residents of these benchmark countries, one could be struck by the fact that, despite their racial, geographical, and other differences, they all look alike. One could trace something even visually common in them. For the first time, when I was in China, I noticed that people of different nationalities, regions, races, and generations look alike, and I recognised elderly Soviet people in the facial features, manners, hairstyles, and behaviour of the older generation of Chinese. In turn, certain European and American features of psyche, and behaviour, and even the facial features of Europeans and Americans, can be traced in the younger generation of Chinese. People from Switzerland and Singapore, Australia and Denmark, Canada and Holland, Sweden and Hong Kong, New Zealand and Ireland look similar today, not because they are rich and developed people, but because they are happy.

When visiting Belarus in July 2015, French actor Gerard Depardieu shared his impressions of the country in an interview: "I see here farms, sown fields, meadows, forests. It resembles a small Switzerland." Resembles? Only the decoding of Belarus would make it possible in the future to resort to a different analogy, comparing not two areas with a similar climate and nature, but two societies, and people inhabiting these areas. This would help to replace "Belarus resembles Switzerland" with "Belarusians resemble the Swiss."

CHAPTER 9

THE WORLD OF 2030

One of the mistakes futurologists make is in saying that everything is going to be different in future; that nature, the cultural environment, and human psychology and physiology will change. Well, this is not the case. Humans will most likely survive by adapting to most, if not all, challenges. Costs could arise due to the high speed of adaptation which would affect human mentality, behaviour, and roles in the world. Another mistake is to forecast that certain developments will happen in 10-15 years, while they can occur much earlier and become somewhat regular and trivial by that time. For instance, back in 2005, few could have predicted the emergence of YouTube, Twitter, Facebook, iPhone, Kindle, Skype, or LinkedIn within a year or two, with the products of these companies consuming nearly all our free time. And the worst mistake is to assert that some events of the past will never happen again: that there will be no natural disasters, epidemics (if it is not plague, then it will be bird flu, Ebola, COVID-19 or another disease), wars, revolutions, or the creation and disappearance of countries, brands, and 'eternal' companies.

Forecasts can be made in different ways. For instance, by extrapolating history along the trajectory of the trends observed, or by analysing the fundamental causes of developments, and projecting the dynamics of meaningful patterns. The world of 2030 is very easy to predict. It can be argued that, due to further growth, the future world will look like today's advanced countries, with the global average catching up. It is likely that the cultural values of the North and West European countries, the US, Canada, Australia, New Zealand, Singapore, Hong Kong, and other countries with a high level of human and economic development, will, on average, become the benchmarks guiding the world in the pursuit of a bright future.

The key question is whether the world's economic growth can be sustained until 2030. Whether the world, on average, will be catching up with the current leaders, or rolling back to the lagging nations. A fundamental study in this area is the forecast covering a period of 100 years, which was made by John Keynes back in 1930. In his book *Economic Possibilities for our Grandchildren*, the British economist predicted that the standard of living would grow 4 to 8 times within 100 years. This, combined with the expected increase in the world population (estimated by the UN to grow from 7.3 billion in 2015 to 8.5 billion in 2030, and to 9.8 billion in 2050), its aging, improved life expectancy (by an average of 2 to 3 years, from 67 to 70 years), and correspondingly higher retirement age, urbanisation (60% of the population will live in the cities that will ensure half of the world's GDP growth), and growth of the world's average labour productivity (estimated by the Ministry of Economic Development of Russia at 2% per year), suggests that the world economy will grow by 2030. PwC forecasts that the average annual world GDP growth will exceed 3%, and China will be the world's largest economy by 2030.

China is the main source of acceleration and slowdown in the world economy.

Based on current trends, the US, the EU, China, and Japan will remain the key drivers of acceleration of the world's economy by 2030. According to different estimates, the contribution of India, Brazil, and Canada will augment this. It is the country-specific perspective where the greatest uncertainty lies, owing to the rapid and not always understandable growth of China's influence on the world economy. In recent years, China has generated a 30% increase in the growth of the global economy and it has become a main trading partner for 124 out of 197 countries of the world. Accordingly, the sustainable development of China's economy may become a determinant of the world development scenario by 2030.

In the 1990s and 2000s, China's economy expanded at an average annual rate of 10-11%. Among the main reasons are its emerged freedom of entrepreneurship, openness and attractiveness to foreign investors, price liberalisation, low salaries (USD 30-70 per month), managed exchange rate, expanding domestic market, privatisation, restructuring of state-owned enterprises, government lending to infrastructure, and real estate construction. The slowdown of China's economy to 8%, 7%, and nearly 6%, in the 2010s, is explained by its demand restructuring (closure of surplus productions), capital outflows, increases in income (in 2016, the average monthly salary exceeded USD 700, reaching USD 1,000-1,500 in some provinces), measures taken to deleverage the government debt (by different estimates, it is more than 200% of GDP), population aging

(China will have 200 million senior citizens by 2030, double the amount in 2010), and its anti-corruption programme.

Overall, the principal cause of the acceleration and slowdown of China's economy is linked, not so much to the level of freedom of entrepreneurship, but rather to the rate of changes in the level of its liberalisation and openness. With regard to the future of China's economy, it is important to recall the irony of the forecast of Nobel Memorial Prize laureate in Economic Sciences, Paul Samuelson. In 1961, in his famous textbook, *Economics*, he predicted that the USSR would surpass the US in terms of its national income level, and that this would definitely have happened by 1997. The forecast of the economist did not change, even in the publication of his book's 1980 edition; it was only adjusted for the 2002 and 2012.

Politics is a major source of unpredictability in the future, both at the national and international level.[170]

The key risk of the downward pressure on the world economy is associated with national economic policies – import substitution, trade and currency wars, strengthening of state controls, anticorruption efforts, defaults, and structural economic reforms.[171][172] The undereducated and manipulated public may fall into populism and demagoguery offering simple answers and solutions. The protection against that, is a high proportion of the middle class (generally people with higher education). Income growth, emerging opportunities for mass higher education, and ICT use to increase the transparency and credibility of elections, will reduce the political risk. According to various estimates, the global middle class will have grown by 3 billion people by 2030. In addition, the focus on the protection of human rights and the democratisation of politics will become an increasingly obvious global trend accompanying the growth of the world economy. A loss of the common agenda among major countries to address global challenges, forms an unstable and unpredictable, rather than multipolar, world. Owing to this political unpredictability, capital will be seeking stable markets, repatriating to developed countries, and widening the gap between developed and developing countries, and global income inequality will ensue. But even the pursuit of prudent policies does not guarantee the opportunity for developing countries to catch up with developed ones. Lagging in technical areas becomes insurmountable for developing countries in the current conditions. In this regard, ensuring that the growth of developing countries can catch up would require not only strengthening their domestic research (for instance, an increase in their R&D funding), but would also mean taking steps such as openness, imports, imitation, and the creation of conditions for freedom of creativity and innovation.

Pace is the key characteristic of the period up to 2030.

Pace will create a qualitatively new environment, largely due to the intensification of Moore's law. Many events occur, information appears, and technologies arise, at a pace beyond understanding and explanation. The only solution would be to absorb them in their conventional forms, much as people perceive electricity simply as light instead of a flow of electric charge, or the internet as a newsfeed, e-mail, and social media, instead of as a fibre-optic network. High-frequency technologies in the financial sector, exchange trade electronic systems (which are still used to make 70% of all transactions in the US and half the transactions in Great Britain) will render these sectors beyond the comprehension of the popular majority, converting them virtually into a roulette game where the house always wins.[173]

According to the forecast of Raymond Kurzweil, Google Director of Engineering, there will be a boom in industrial nanotechnology by 2030. By then, computers will have exceeded the power of the human brain, solar energy will have satisfied the entire human demand for energy, a mass market of gadget implants will have been established, and wires will have been eradicated in any area of activity.[174] As a consequence of technological development acceleration, the world of 2030 will be a place where emotionality will be increasingly inferior to rationality, where the cultural matrix will become a technological one, with more productive, efficient software, and robots making fewer mistakes than humans. A few hundred years ago, several generations of people would be needed for the introduction and complete adoption of new technologies, while adaptation in the 20th century was completed within a single generation. More recently, it has taken 5-10 years for a new technology to be absorbed, become outdated, and be replaced with a new one. Consequently, old habits and long-term cultural values are blurred under the weight of the imperative to follow the rapidly emerging new technologies.

Unemployment is the main economic threat of the future.

The technological matrix lays the ground for constant structural unemployment. This subject has always been of concern to economists. As early as 1821, David Ricardo studied "the influence of machinery on the interests of the different classes of society", and particularly the working class. Nobel Memorial Prize laureate in Economic Sciences, Wassily Leontief, predicted that robots would replace humans in industry just as tractors replaced horses in agriculture. Noteworthy, for instance, is the reduction of the physical quantity of horses in the US in the 20th century: 21.5 million horses in 1900, 26.5 million in 1915, and 3.1 million in 1960.[175] In this regard, there was a shift in jobs from agriculture to industry. To use Great Britain as an illustration, the share of employment in agriculture at that time was 22%, while at present it is less than 1%.[176] Then, jobs began to shift from industry to services, and in future, the current, traditional jobs will be at risk of disappearing. Robots, which need neither wages nor trade unions, are the principal human competitor in the labour market. Low-skilled student and trainee work, such as document cataloguing, can already be performed by machines. The work of housebuilders can be performed by 3D printers, couriers by drones, waiters in sushi bars by conveyors, and paper menus become electronic. Nurses will be replaced by robots – something already practised in Japan. In a number of large supermarkets, for instance in Wal-Mart, robots work night shifts to set out goods on shelves, while 'smart' electronic security systems substitute guards.

The job of a driver, which is most common today, is likely to disappear as well. Self-driving cars — along with unmanned airplanes — will become as commonplace as unmanned trams and trains, which minimises the human error factor that accounts for 90% of traffic accidents. Google self-driving cars have already been cruising the roads of California for ten years. The concept of an unmanned vehicle was introduced as early as 1939, by General Motors at the New York International Automobile Show. However, the implementation of this idea was only launched with the advent of sensors and computers, and by 2030 it will become a widespread phenomenon, due to the development of the Internet of Things. In general, the development of the Internet of Things over years will allow the programming and speeding up of all low-productive manufacturing processes.

Unemployment can occur among highly skilled workers as well. The skills and knowledge of engineers, and doctors of sciences, can be programmed and adapted for use by common people, conducting in-home high-precision operations. Translation (including simultaneous) into any language will become generally available. Even today, computer programmes test knowledge and evaluate plagiarism, which, however, can lead to people trying to adjust their knowledge to programmes, rather than preparing themselves for real life situations. They try to deceive the computer remotely, and in response, identification and face recognition software emerges.

There are technologies in sight that will replace the emotionality of a person. Software for writing poetry, inspiring speeches, producing paintings, and composing music, has already been created. All of this leads to the devaluation of traditional human skills. Navigation skills have already been replaced by the GPS, mental calculation by the calculator, intuition by big data, and instincts by algorithms. Moreover, big data sets that are difficult for humans to 'digest', increasingly generate infoglut, and this raises the value of small – processed, individual, and subject-oriented - data.[177]

According to some estimates, robots are already potentially able to replace 47% of the workforce in the US, 35% in Great Britain, and 49% in Japan.[178] Since robots could replace practically all human qualities today, the emergence of artificial intelligence by 2030 seems possible. 42% of computer scientists predict the emergence of artificial intelligence by 2030, 25% by 2050, 20% by 2100, and only 2% say that it will never appear.[179] For its part, Bank of America Merrill Lynch predicts that, by 2030, artificial intelligence will reduce global labour costs by USD 9 trillion, and health care costs by USD 8 trillion. In 2015, investment in artificial intelligence ecosystems reached a record USD 8.5 billion, four times the 2010 amount, and 16% more than in 2014, while the overall investment in the technological sector dropped by 3% in 2015.[180]

Spare time is the prime resource of the future.

People will have more spare time both at work and at home. Even now, technologies give people more spare time, substituting humans with washing and dishwashing machines, microwave ovens and numerous other appliances that do the housework. Virtually all the routine procedures of human household activity will be accelerated as the Internet of Things' technologies evolve: programming morning, lunch time, evening, and night. All this adds value to the remaining housework and provides an opportunity to rest and recover, improve productivity, devote oneself to creative activities and innovations, and improve health, which, together with emerging new drugs, contributes to an increase in life expectancy.

However, a person may fail to take advantage of these opportunities and spend their spare time on virtual, rather than real life, computer games, the internet, pornography, alcohol, drugs, and gambling. In this regard, the entertainment industry, including the internet, becomes particularly important. The escape from reality into the virtual world provides a means of raising self-esteem, a feeling of being at the same level as entertainers, the public, respected people, and professionals. Anonymous recommendations on how to address important life and financial challenges, can be received in this virtual environment during chat sessions with people represented by accounts set up under fake names, whose input acquires a value that equates to the advice of scientists and professionals. This leads to irrational decision-making. This unhealthy environment obviously poses a threat to humankind. If people cannot cope with it, they then need outside assistance in the form of restrictive programmes inducing sensible thinking and prompting rational behaviour.

New business models are the main source of development for the global economy.

The extensive growth of the world economy has reached a certain limit, and India is likely to be among the few countries using this model by 2030. The rest of the world will move from growth to development and the sources of the latter are difficult to predict, since they will be new. Joseph Schumpeter gave a vivid description of the difference between economic growth and economic development: "Add successively as many mail coaches as you please, but you will never get a railway".

In future, the business environment will change due to the development of technologies and big data. It will generate new and unpredictable business models. Even now, entities such as Uber, Airbnb, and Amazon, suddenly appear in traditional sectors. They are successful, however sometimes it seems that they have little understanding, and no traditions, of the transport sector, hotel business, or cinematography. The titans of the respective sectors, in turn, have an opportunity to fundamentally change themselves and their activities. For instance, banks, electronic trading platforms matching buyers and sellers, companies that own social media, and mobile operators all enjoy the competitive advantage of big data sets. Drawing on this advantage, they can start any sort of business by providing services for which customers do not yet feel the need. The high stock prices of companies such as Alibaba and Facebook can probably be attributed to investors' expectations that big data are likely to be used in ways that have not yet been discovered.

The success of blockchains and bitcoins may inspire the use of these models in other areas of business and public administration. A multicurrency system based on the circulation of national, international, and crypto, currencies seems likely to become reality by 2030, since

Amazon and eBay have already started to accept bitcoins as means of payment, and a number of major countries have announced the introduction of their own crypto currencies. It is notable that the unpredictable and rapid emergence of new business models results in the mental and physical lagging behind of public administration. The state will not only fail to keep up with the emerging business models, but will also be unable to fully understand the way they work, and where and how they accumulate profits. This will lead to an increasing occurrence of unregulated business spheres, as was previously the case with offshore activities, which will emerge and collapse before the state can work out a comprehensive and effective regulatory mechanism.

Environmental challenges represent the main risk for human existence on the planet.

Population growth, life quality improvement and getting comfortable with it, urbanisation, and technological acceleration, all lead to an unprecedented pressure being placed on nature, such as the growth of consumption of natural resources, including forest and fresh water resources, increased fertilizer usage, depletion of hydrocarbon reserves, significant tropical deforestation, the major deterioration of mariculture, abnormal ranges of seasonal temperatures, global warming (advantageous for northern countries), and air pollution (urban air, in particular). At the same time, the capacity of coal power plants (the main source of air pollution) has been growing rather than decreasing in recent years. In 2000, the global coal-fired power generation capacity was 1,132 GW, and in 2014 – 1,980 GW.[181]

The current environmental situation is considered unmatched in the history of the planet. It is therefore impossible to predict the future behaviour and responses of nature.[182] The only thing that remains uncontested is that environmental risks will have become more pressing, and their mitigation will be the challenge for the incumbent developed countries which are equipped with the requisite technologies and universal global values, rather than developing countries like China and India. For instance, the United States has made commitments to reduce greenhouse gas emissions by 26-28% until 2025, and South Korea by 37% until 2030. Still, it is not enough. Even after these planned reductions, emissions in South Korea will be 81% higher in 2030 than in 1990. In this regard, non-governmental organisations, empowered by new technologies, will likely be the ones to take the initiative in addressing environmental challenges.

How to Adapt to the New Technological Matrix

First, there must be optimism, a positive attitude towards changes.

It is essential to understand that accelerating technologies are created and designed for the benefit, not the detriment, of humans. Therefore, they will be focused, in the first place, on improving people's overall productivity, satisfying their needs and desires, making individuals more competitive, healthy and happy. For instance, even today, there are R&D products that can identify genes related to a particular predisposition to a certain occupation, profession, hobby, disease, stress, schizophrenia, suicidal behaviour, alcohol abuse, or drug addiction. This enables the programming of life; the recommendation of appropriate drugs, climate, or diet, plans to stay clear of bottlenecks in one's 'destiny' and to commit oneself entirely to personal fulfilment in a particular area to which the individual is most predisposed.

Artificial intelligence can be aimed at making a breakthrough in science, processing lots of research and big data, performing experiments to address climate issues, and produce life-prolonging medicines. According to speeches given by US President, Barack Obama, in 2016, America will be able to solve the problem of cancer by the 2030s. All of this implies that by the 2030s, the above mentioned technologies will have become widespread and accessible for all, rather than episodic and experimental. Humans might be unable to handle the changes that affect them, and, therefore, individual health support programmes and personalised sets of medicines will probably be needed to put them in a favourable and constructive mood. Thus, new technologies will provide new positive opportunities for people, and it is important to feel optimistic about making initial changes in one's lifestyle to be able to adapt to the new technological matrix.

Second, for many people adaptation will be a natural phenomenon.

Several generations of people have already been born into an environment of accelerated technological development. They have adopted new systems since birth and been unaware of any different way of life. Therefore, they take it for granted without investing time or significant effort. Furthermore, this type of technological environment has every reason to be considered a public good. Since major technological discoveries have been funded with tax money, society is the main investor and has the right to universal access to new technologies.

Of course, adaptation will not be natural for everyone. Educational programmes for older generations will be needed in response to population ageing, to accelerate their 'digestion' of new technologies and changes. Additionally, education will ultimately reach out to those who previously showed no inclination towards study, and, eventually, this will foster the growth of the middle class. The value of online education will also increase, and the certification awarded will progressively gain value, since this education will be increasingly recognized (people will be ready to pay more for it) and society (employers, offline education institutions).

Third, the time gap between education and work should be shortened to catch up with the accelerated technological development.

The traditional model — which implies that with earlier and more education one acquires longer and better dividends — will become ineffective. Theoretical knowledge, acquired over extended periods of time and confirmed by university diplomas or academic degrees, will increasingly yield to practical skills acquired through short-term corporate training sessions. The real sector and companies will no longer be able to wait until the education system evaluates the prospects of the labour market, adjusts its curricula and, 4-5 years later, offers a specialist seen by the education system as suitable. Today, an increasing number of university graduates in developed countries are employed every year in jobs outside their field of specialisation, while jobs are increasingly taken up worldwide by people without even secondary education.

There will be a considerable rejuvenation of productive years in the information age. It has been established that the age of 20 is the peak, when a person can acquire and digest information at maximum speed. The perceptual speed starts to decline after 20 years of age.[183] Accordingly, the younger generation most rapidly mastering new technologies will face the dilemma of choosing between university and business. Talented students may establish businesses and, as this has occurred with increasing frequency, self-actualize, and become young billionaires, thanks to their start-ups.

Accelerated education does not mean that middle-aged and older people will not learn. A new education model will include many continuing short-term training sessions on high-demand practical subjects aimed at addressing specific problems. In this regard, the most valuable formal training would be fostering and developing skills such as intellectual curiosity, self-motivation, aptitude, ability, and even the habits of learning fast, absorbing knowledge, and immediately putting it into practice. Success stories of new continuing education models already exist in advanced countries. For instance, since January 2016, every citizen of Singapore aged over 25 can receive a subsidy of SGD 500 (USD 345) to pay for training courses offered by 500 designated organisations, including universities, online agencies, etc. Besides, an additional subsidy of up to 90% is granted to residents over 40 years of age. The original budget of this education programme was SGD 600 million, to be increased to SGD 1 billion in three years.[184]

Fourth, a job would have to be created, not looked for.

Competing with robots will require not only continuing education, but also improvisation, enterprise, a constant quest for new things, and getting rid of stereotypes, habits, traditions and all the other things a machine can imitate. Unlike gained employment, a devised job will be a pleasure, will provide good incentives, and give rise to a desire to get a client or outperform a competitor, because, above all, it is interesting and 'cool'. There are several studies that refute the threat of structural unemployment and show that workplace automation ensures cost and price reduction, growth in demand, and change of preferences. As a result, output increases and more jobs are created, and this is confirmed by empirical evidence.[185] Whereas previously, a person could find a job in a different sphere, there will simply be no low-skilled positions in the context of global IT development in all spheres. Besides, these studies are based on the data of the opened demographic window, with a high proportion of young people quickly adapting to changes and new technologies. Technologies, indeed, create entirely new jobs; however, 60-year-old employees are unlikely to learn new skills quickly. Therefore, the primary bearers of cultural values – the senior and middle-aged generations – are the most vulnerable to the new technological matrix.

Fifth, global values will help overcome cultural barriers to adaptation to the technological matrix.

The generation of millennials, raised at the time of globalisation, tends to rely on the universal values of the global cultural matrix. This strengthens such qualities as cosmopolitanism, a sense of ownership of the country and the planet, openness, decentralisation of decisions and federalism, pluralism, avoidance of dogmas and stereotypes, tolerance, self-control in the context of impoliteness and discourtesy, and human rights protection, including gender, ethnic, and religious equality.

Liberal values will be increasingly strengthened, due to the influence of expanding urbanisation: as one German proverb goes, "The air of the town gives freedom". At the same time, new generations, raised in the environment of the internet, will be prone to narcissism. This will distort family values, create conditions for an increase in divorces, polygamy, civil, non-traditional, and late marriages (the latter would encourage a longer period of education). In general, if routine work is performed by artificial intelligence, inertial and habitual cultural thinking and behaviour will be increasingly replaced by automatic fulfilment. But this does not mean that the cultural matrix will be completely replaced by the technological one (as was the case when the atomic bomb was invented and used against people in Japan). Human values will continue to dominate and manage technologies.

Sixth, the global economic code will be focused on savings.

Further income growth will require time to manage and enjoy the wealth. This will form an orientation to saving and preserving the present, rather than shaping the future. A certain saturation of material wealth will shift the focus to the value of human communication with families, parents, children (biological and adopted), and friends, as well as to reading, education, and so forth. The value of professional self-realisation and satisfying personal interests will rise. In turn, pleasure in the job (working from home or outside home) will generate higher numbers of workaholics. Thus, the economic component may lose its weight in the matrix of cultural values and be replaced with the orientation to individualism, public and political spheres, health, leisure, etc.

In recent years, the economic global code has been mainly consumption-oriented and debt-financed.[186][187] This resulted in an overheating of the markets of real estate, cars, education, and other goods and services financed with loans, and subsequently led to a debt bubble. The threat of structural unemployment, fear of being replaced by robots or retiring early with a relatively low income, and weakening consumer values, will stimulate savings and restrain economic growth.

In order to boost consumption and economic growth, the government should probably raise pensions, unemployment benefits, and shift taxation from consumption and income to savings, that is, to capital and accumulated wealth. Additionally, it may necessitate the wide-scale introduction of fixed state support payments to citizens, or the so-called universal basic income related to social security benefits, for instance, an annual payment of USD 10,000 to maintain a certain standard of living and consumption, or to give a chance of self-realization in another sphere in response to technological unemployment. Such an experiment was launched in Finland on 1 January 2017, Holland has scheduled it for the period ahead, while Switzerland called it quits, fearing an influx of migrants.

Seventh, by 2030 mankind will have come to understand the importance of the ecological situation.

A large-scale global opinion-gathering exercise, conducted by the UN in 2015 and related to the importance and ranking of values, finds that people in highly developed countries view climate change as the 10th most important issue out of a list of 16 that includes health care, jobs, political freedom, internet access, etc., while in developing countries, climate change is 16th out of 16.[188] Such an attitude is explained when consideration is given to the priority issues in politics and the authorities' ability to respond to environmental challenges without external aid.

Given the anticipated environmental degradation, the political attention to these problems is also expected to increase, and hence an updating of the global cultural matrix will be forthcoming. Even today, such measures as alternative energy (the share of alternative sources of energy is 70% in Sweden and almost 40% in Germany), incentives offered by the state to promote energy saving, 'smart meters', restricted use of vehicles, application of advanced materials, new generations of nuclear reactors, and expansion of the market of greenhouse gas emission permits, as well as fines and taxes on polluting industries, produce a meaningful, but still insufficient, effect. The broad awareness of our responsibility for the planet is likely to be realised by mankind by 2030. However, we cannot ignore the risk that this would be too late. Thus, no matter how futuristic it sounds, further environmental degradation due to technological upheaval will apparently encourage humans to find a different life environment. For instance, several countries have declared the colonization of the Moon and Mars by 2030 as an alternative living environment.

Eighth, people have already begun preparations for 2030.

In 2015, the United Nations General Assembly adopted a resolution "Transforming our world: the 2030 Agenda for Sustainable Development".[189] The resolution lays out 17 Sustainable Development Goals:

1) end poverty;
2) end hunger;
3) ensure healthy lives and promote wellbeing;
4) ensure quality education;
5) achieve gender equality;
6) ensure the availability and sustainable management of water and sanitation;
7) ensure access to affordable and sustainable energy;
8) promote economic growth and decent work;
9) build infrastructure, promote industrialization, and foster innovation;
10) reduce inequality;
11) sustainable cities and human settlements;
12) sustainable consumption and production patterns;
13) combat climate change;
14) conserve marine ecosystems;
15) protect terrestrial ecosystems;
16) peace, justice, and effective institutions;
17) partnerships for sustainable development.

This is neither a declaration, nor a dream. This is real, as were the UN Millennium Development Goals, declared in 2000 and achieved by 2015. Each of the above listed goals of the 2030 Agenda has a set of indicators and tools, and they are based on human capital, which will prevail over technological capital. Therefore, the Sustainable Development Goals bring hope, since they suggest a practical survival mechanism for humankind in the new technological matrix, and the preservation of universal human values.

The visualization of the future does not imply a precise and detailed picture of what is going to happen. Just as, long ago, one could accurately predict the invention of an airplane, although, at that moment, it was probably difficult to imagine that an airplane would not have to flap its wings in flight. Nevertheless, in spite of the risk of committing a futurologist mistake, it can be predicted that things are going to be different in 2030, and the national cultural matrix will be significantly reshaped, if not replaced, by the technological one.

How will the Belarusian cultural matrix and the global technological matrix match up in 2030?

On the one hand, *the inertia forecast concerning the future causes pragmatic pessimism.* Belarus becomes incapable of closing the gap in its innovation development on its own, given the apparent global technological trends created without Belarus' input. Just as in other developing countries, Belarus' competitive advantage of low wages is offset by the best ratio of costs and labour productivity provided by robots. All this condemns the country to a long period of economic depression and a relative slowdown of improvement, if not deterioration, of living standards. Structural unemployment could become a confrontation line in the ideological struggle between the cultural and the technological matrices. This, in turn, could revive and consolidate populist, socialist and communist, ideas. The result is that the cultural matrix in Belarus eventually has the prospect of prevailing over the technological matrix, thereby reinforcing the negative economic trend.

On the other hand, *hopes for rational thinking and behaviour, in the context of the new technological reality, are encouraging.* The recognition of challenges, and the lowering of the threshold of national pride in order to overcome cultural barriers, open the way for economic growth. As noted previously, a self-sustaining decoding of Belarus' economy seems unlikely. Waiting for a generational shift and evolutionary cultivation of universal values in the environment of accelerated technological development wastes time. Consequently, the foreign investment-induced decoding of Belarus' economy, accompanied by social dialogue, facilitation, institutionalisation, and so forth, would eventually make it possible to develop new features of the Belarusian matrix that may ensure the incorporation and integration of the national and international matrices.

CONCLUSION

When I was at school, we once got a home assignment for the summer: to read a book of our own choice and write its summary. My father then slipped me the recently released *Boys in Zinc* by Svetlana Alexievich.[190] I remember that book, as well as my mark for the summary, like a bright flash. When I opened my notebook, returned by the teacher, I saw that each page was red with corrections of my grammar mistakes. I leafed to the end, expecting to see devastating and unflattering comments, but saw an 'A minus'.

I wanted to give this book the title *Because I Decided So*, but changed it to 'we' in order to be optimistic, and avoid misunderstanding as to what stands behind 'I'. Maybe 'I' is more correct, because Belarusians are disunited, every man for himself. With the undeveloped, internal consolidating element of Belarusian society, statehood becomes external. Up to a certain level of development, statehood consolidates, stimulating economic growth, but then the economy falls into a trap and moves in circles. To shift from 'I' to 'we', from individualism to solidarity (and not to collective egoism), we must develop the aspirations of certainty, courage, openness, tolerance, and pluralism. These values can unite the Belarusian society, create the 'we', stimulate innovation, and help the economy get out of the 'middle income trap'.

After writing this book, I had hoped to have a pleasant feeling of ease associated with approaching the truth and unveiling the secret of Belarus' behavioural economy. But, there are still some disturbing doubts. They are associated with the understanding that the scientific provability is reduced due to trying to explain to the international reader some complex processes in simple terms, using analogies and historical examples. Enthusiasm sometimes impairs knowledge. Expert appraisal, scientific intuition, and mental modelling seem to prevail in this book, while statistics, sociological measurements, and calculations are fudged to fit the picture. As a result, the behavioural economics of Belarus appears to be a theory with half-open eyes. And it indeed is. In Belarus' behavioural economics, emotions, words, and memories of the past, prevail over (sometimes unexpectedly awakening) reasoning, figures, and a vision of the future. The main principle of making a decision is "not to make things worse than they were". It is more important than "to make things right and better." Moreover, the reference point of 'were' is very relative and dynamic, and reflects not only economics, but also culture, politics, and expectations. Since decisions are made based on feelings, intuition, and instincts, it can be stated that everything is accounted for in behavioural economics, with information absorbed from all sources; everything that has been heard, seen, felt, read, and calculated, which creates an aggregate picture of sometimes random things. In this regard, in Belarus' behavioural economics, one could never know for sure what can outweigh and influence the decision, and whether that decision is final. This is its main feature, the barrier, and the reason for decoding for the sake of sustainable growth.

I always asked myself if decoding is really possible. If the economic reforms i.e. the 'financial diet' doesn't work, how would decoding work? Any diets, not only financial ones, usually do not work because we don't have enough discipline to be rational, or because we decided to do nothing and to be irrational. Only when a disaster strikes, do we have to become smart. But decoding is also possible without a disaster. The influence of the cultural matrix is not absolute. It can always be mitigated by books, the internet, communication, or music from headphones. Strangely enough, this is the key to decoding! The change of the information and cultural environment.

In this regard, decoding is possible in two ways.

First, as Karl Marx said, "the people must be taught to be terrified of itself in order to give it courage". The horrors of the Great Patriotic War became deeply rooted in Belarusians, shaping their attitude towards the war. But, the human toll of the Russian Revolution of 1917, the Civil War, the collectivisation/Holodomor, and the 'Great Purge' of 1937-1938, was higher than the losses of the USSR during the Second World War. Belarus will go around in circles until it acknowledges the dark past.

Second, one could rely on the good things that we are periodically exposed to and transmit. I was an eyewitness to my father being reprogrammed when he was listening to the jammed broadcasts of the *Voice of America*, and reading *Novy Mir* magazine in the 1980s. These were replaced by the *NTV* channel in the 1990s, and then by the *Echo Moskvy* radio station in the 2000s. He was the one periodically pushing me towards decoding, just as the whole Belarusian cultural matrix is pushing itself to that.

After writing this book, I am surprised at myself for being able to accomplish this within such a short time. How did I turn from economist to sociologist? What do I really preach? The answer is the true nature of human behaviour, which is freedom. In this book, I unconsciously offer the path for economic freedom. *Because We Decided So* deals with the question of how to bring freedom and responsibility to cultural values for the benefit of the nation and its future, how to get away from the irrational, how to cultivate economic freedom and prove that to be free means to be rational. There is an old joke: "What do you want? Freedom! But you are free, as you are not in jail!" In Belarus, the historical prison-like closeness, corresponding rhetoric, culture, and news background, preserve the negative social incentives inherited by society, make people value the present, and focus on survival and adaptation. Such values maintain fear, and are predominant over freedom and initiative. Courage is a product of certainty and is expressed in the unanimous understanding of "what is good" and "what is bad", and in not allowing the freedom to choose non-freedom. In turn, certainty is a product of the mind. And to make the mind fearless, it is necessary to free science and education from dogmas. One can start decoding to move towards freedom with anything, the main thing is to instil trust. People must believe in the irreversibility of change, and it is essential to convince not only oneself and one's friends. Long-term public trust is formed not within one's own circle, but as trust towards strangers. This is the foundation for building a civil society, the emergence of 'we', which will maintain the steadfast demand for sustainable development.

At the end of this book, I'll take the risk to forecast the future of Belarus and its economy, which can be distilled to two scenarios.

Scenario one: the past is unknown; the future is predetermined.

In this case, there is continued orientation towards the Soviet past and a future of inertia. The search for solutions to the ever-reappearing problems of the past makes this past changeable and unknown. Ambiguous, sometimes contradictory appraisals of yesterday's events disorient, support doublethink and permanent uncertainty, accumulate fatigue, and push towards conservatism. As a result, the past does not change *de facto*, preserving its uncertainty and not changing the future. The impact of such a scenario on the economy is predictable. There would be no new points of growth, old ones would be exhausted, and the debt overhang would create a burden for Belarus' economy, which would generate inertia growth of 1% per year.

The forecast once offered back in 2015[191] showed that, with an average annual GDP growth of 1%, by 2030, Belarus would be lagging 20 years behind its neighbouring countries (Poland, Estonia, and Russia) in terms of its level of economic development. But, this could have been an optimistic forecast. Over the past several years, Belarus has lagged behind itself and rolled several years back. Nevertheless, the comfortable doom of going in circles could be more suitable for Belarusians than a straightforward reaction to humiliating impoverishment. And based on the position "because I decided so", everyone should be held accountable for that.

Scenario two: the past is defined; the future is unknown.

Decoding is possible through introduction of international universal values, public dialogue, assessment of the past, institutionalisation, law enforcement, educational paternalism, social nudge, and political transformation. Decoding would save the Belarusian cultural matrix. The emergence of new features, such as certainty, courage, openness, tolerance, and pluralism, would give hope that the future is unknown, and there is a chance associated with mobilising public will and competence to bring the best international practices to the country, and capital which would create new points of growth unknown today. Under such a scenario, the average annual growth of the Belarusian economy could be different, say 5% or 7%, outstripping the average world economy growth.

However, it should be understood that, in this case, no miracle would occur by 2030 either. Belarus would not close but would reduce the gap. And, most importantly, the orientation may change. There would be the chance to catch up, not with neighbouring countries but with advanced economies. There will be new benchmarks: with such average annual rates of growth, Belarus would still be lagging behind by twenty or thirty years, but compared to Switzerland, Denmark, and Singapore. And this is a different cultural matrix, trend, and reality. This is already the sustainable recovery of Belarus' economy, decoding with transition from behavioural to classical economics, moving to a trajectory of 'one hundred years of growth'. Thus, a different society would be formed, as it would not be the sum of weakly-linked elements — "because I decided so" combining into the sovereign 'we', – but a wide-reaching public 'we' based on the self-conscious "because *we* decided so."

My jealous straight-A classmates were asking me and the teacher why my summary full of grammar mistakes was highly rated. I waved them off saying "because the teacher decided so". But the teacher entered into a dialogue with them, saying that, in this case, the content was more important than the form, that the purity of thinking was more important than the purity of writing; explaining, teaching, and decoding, both them and himself.

Acknowledgements

This book came out of the stress created when my father, Valentin Alexandrovich Rudy, passed away in 2017. So it's dedicated to him, and my mother Vera Antonovna Kruglyanina. Sometimes I put unfair blame on them, trying to explain that our behavioural economy exists and evolves so slowly because *they* decided so. But it's not completely true. I see my father's and mother's judgments and unconscious behaviour in me. So it's all because *we* decided so.

Special thanks should go to those who discouraged me from writing and publishing this book, and then were usually the first to express congratulations on its publication – these are the closest and most emotionally involved people. I couldn't be more grateful to my wife Elena and two sons Anton and Ilya. They keep on waiting to have family time, when the book is over until a new book comes to my mind and steals me from them.

This book is a brief edition of a more extensive study in Russian — "Because We Decided So: Behavioural Economics of Belarus and its Decoding" — prepared by sociologists, lawyers and economists.[192] This abridged English version would be different without the support and contribution of some of my colleagues from the Institute of Sociology of the National Academy of Science, Research Centre IPM, Belarus State Economic University: Irina Lashuk, Igor Kotlyarov, Elena Taranova, Natalia Sechko, Natalia Denisova, and Daria Urban.

Special credit should be given to the reviewers, who read the manuscript and shared their valuable comments, which have been reflected in the book, and which changed it, including: Yulyia Chernyavskaya, Yury Zisser (passed away), Yuri Tserlukevich, Andrey Movchan, Yuriy Gorodnichenko, Zhu Ning, Arkadiy Dobkin, and last, but not least, Belarusian Nobel Prize laureate in Literature, Svetlana Alexievich.

In this book, it is essential to extend thanks to the long-standing mentors, whose thoughts, words, and actions have left a profound imprint, thus influencing any further research. They are Vladimir Shimov, Professor, Doctor of Economics, and Mikhail Myasnikovich, Corresponding Member, Professor, Doctor of Economics.

It is also important to name the person who supported Russian publication, ex-UNDP coordinator in Belarus, Sanaka Samarasinha. There would be no English version without the Russian one.

The sources of academic inspiration for writing this book include the research of the founders of behavioural economics: Nobel Memorial Prize laureates in Economic Sciences, Daniel Kahneman, Amos Tversky, and Richard Thaler, as well as legal scholar Cass Sunstein.[193][194][195][196]

This book was published during difficult time for Belarus nation, which started in August of 2020, and by now it's hard to predict where it goes. But no matter where it finally comes, it's because we (Belarusians) decided so. So I am grateful for this book to Belarusians.

Kiryl Rudy
August 2020

NOTES

1 Kapelushnikov R. (2013). Behavioral Economy and New Paternalism. (In Russian) Moscow, Publishing House: High School of Economics, 2013.
2 Lewis M. (2017). The Undoing Project. A Friendship That Change Our Minds / W. W. Norton & Company, New York, 2017 – 362 p.
3 Weber M. (1990). Selected Works (In Russian) / M. Weber [Electronic Resource]. – 1990. – Mode of access:
http://www.gumer.info/bibliotek_Buks/Sociolog/vebizbr/index.php – time of access: 10.06.2013.
4 Kahneman D. (2013) Thinking, Fast and Slow. / Farrar, Straus and Giroux. New York, 2013. – 499 p.
5 Guiso L., Sapienzia P., Zingales L. (2006). Does Culture Affect Economic Outcomes? - National Bureau of Economic Research. January 2002. Working paper 11999.
6 Barberis N., Thaler R. (2002). A Survey of Behavioral Finance. / NBER, Working Paper 9222, September 2002. – 78 p.
7 Vissing-Jorgensen A. (2003). Perspectives on Behavioral Finance: Does "Irrationality" Disappear with Wealth? Evidence from Expectations and Actions. / NBER Macroeconomic Annual 2003, Volume 18 (2004). Mark Gertler and Kenneth Rogoff editors. Conference held April 4 -5, 2003. Published in July 2004 by the MIT Press, pp. 139 – 208.
8 Bourdieu P. (1998). Structure, Gabitus, Practice. (In Russian) // Journal of Sociology and Social Anthropology. 1998. Part 1. Ed. 2.
9 Bourdieu P. (2007). Physical and Social Areas (In Russian) // Sociology of Social Areas. – Moscow: Institute of Experimental Sociology; 2007. – 288 p.
10 Mlodinow L. (2012). How Your Unconscious Mind Rules Your Behavior. – Vintage Books. A Division of Random House, Inc. New York, 2012. – 260 p.
11 Kahneman D. (2013) Thinkig, Fast and Slow. / Farrar, Straus and Giroux. New York, 2013. – 499 p.
12 Ibid
13 Harvey C., Sticht P. (2001). The International Cost of Capital and Risk Calculator (ICCRC). National Bureau of Economic Research, Cambridge, Massachusetts: 20 p.
14 Treisman D. (2012). The Return: Russia's Journey from Gorbachev to Medvedev. -/ Free Press, 2012. – 544 p.
15 Lewis R.D. (2005). When Cultures Collide: Leading Across Cultures / Nicholas Brealey Publishing, 2005. – 599 p.
16 Hall Edward T. (2000). Understanding Cultural Differences: Germans, French and Americans. / Nicholas Brealey, 2000. – 224 p.
17 Chernyavskay Y. (2010). Belarusians: from "tuteishya" to the nation. (In Russian) – Moscow: FUAinform, 2010. – 512 p.

18 Lacorne D. (2019). The Limits of Tolerance. Enlightenment Values and Religious Fanaticism. / Columbia University Press, 2019. – 280 p.
19 Sharma R. (2016). The Rise and Fall of Nations: Forces of Change in the Post Crisis World. / W.W. Norton & Company, 2016. – 466 p.
20 Zuboff Sh. (2019). The Age of Surveillance Capitalism. – New York: Public Affairs, 2019. – 691 p.
21 Morgenshtern O., Neumann J. (2012). Games Theory and Economic Behavior (In Russian). – Moscow: The Book on Demand, 2012. – 708 p.
22 Harrison L., Huntington S. (2001) Culture Matters: How Values Shape Human Progress. – Basic Books, 2001. – 384 p.
23 Rapaille C. (2015). The Global Code: How a New Culture of Universal Values is Reshaping Business and Marketing. / St. Martin's Press, 2015. – 304 p.
24 Hakamada I. (2017). Personally Yours. (In Russian) – March, 31, 2017. – http://echo.msk.ru/programs/personalnovash/1954016-echo/
25 Banerjee A., Duflo E. (2012). Poor Economics: A Radical Rethinking of the Way to Fight Global Poverty. / Public Affairs, 2012. – 320 p.
26 Friedman T.L. (2016). Thank You for Being Late: An Optimist's Guide to Thriving in the Age of Accelerations. / Farrar, 2016. – 496 p.
27 Weber M. (1930). The Protestant Ethic and the Spirit of Capitalism / M. Weber – London: Allen and Unwin, 1930. – 443 p.
28 Friedman T.L. (2016). Thank You for Being Late: An Optimist's Guide to Thriving in the Age of Accelerations. / Farrar, 2016. – 496 p.
29 Harrison L. (2016). Jews, Confucians, and Protestants Cultural Capital and the End of Multiculturalism (In Russian). – Moscow: "Idea", 2016.
30 Barro R. (2003). International Determinants of Religiosity / R. Barro, R. McCleary // National Bureau of Economic Research [Electronic resource] – 2003. - № 10147. – Mode of access: http://www.nber.org – Date of access: 25.01.2008.
31 Guiso L., Sapienzia P., Zingales L. (2002). People's Opium?: Religion and Economic Attitudes. - National Bureau of Economic Research – 2002. Working Paper № 9237.
32 Tambovcev V B. (2015). Myth about "Cultural Code" in Economic Researches (In Russian). // Voprosy economiki. 2015. №12. C. 85 – 106.
33 Fernandez R. (2010) Does Culture Matter? - Working Paper No. 16277. National Bureau of Economic Research. Cambridge, MA. August 2010. – 44 p.
34 Terracciano A., and others (2005). National Character Does Not Reflect Mean Personality Trait Levels in 49 Countries. // Science. 2005. Oct. 7, 310 (5745), 96 – 100. - https://www.ncbi.nlm.nih.gov/pmc/articles/PMC2775052/
35 Fernandez R. (2010) Does Culture Matter? - Working Paper No. 16277. National Bureau of Economic Research. Cambridge, MA. August 2010. – 44 p.
36 Gladwell M. (2011) Outliers: The Story of Success. – Little, Brown and Company. – New York, 2011. – 336 p.

37 Pinker S. (2003). The Blank Slate: The Modern Denial of Human Nature. / Penguin Books, 2003. – 560 p.
38 Auzan A. (2015). "Path Dependence" Trap (In Russian). / https://www.youtube.com/watch?v=E16qw1nc4tU
39 North D.C., Wallis J.J. & more (2013). Violence and Social Orders: A Conceptual Framework for Interpreting Recorded Human History. – Cambridge University Press, 2013. – 346 p.
40 The Economist. (2016). The Toll of Tariffs. / The Economist, April 16th 2016, p. 60.
41 Harrison L. (2016). Jews, Confucians, and Protestants Cultural Capital and the End of Multiculturalism (In Russian). – Moscow: "Idea", 2016.
42 Hall Edward T. (2000). Understanding Cultural Differences: Germans, French and Americans. / Nicholas Brealey, 2000. – 224 p.
43 ibid.
44 Lewis R.D. (2005). When Cultures Collide: Leading Across Cultures / Nicholas Brealey Publishing, 2005. – 599 p.
45 Levitsky S. (2010). Competitive Authoritarianism: Hybrid Regimes after the Cold War (Problems of International Politics). – Cambridge University Press, 2010. – 536 p.
46 Hayek F.A. (2007). The Road to Serfdom: Text and Documents. – The Definitive Edition. / University of Chicago Press, Chicago. – 283 p.
47 What Features of the Soviets were inherited by Modern Russians (In Russian) (2011). Levada-Center Project "Soviet Simple Man". // https://www.svoboda.org/a/24332717.html
48 Lewis M. (2011). Boomerang: Travels in a New Third World. / W.W.Norton and Company. - New York, 2011. – 224 p.
49 Eco U. (2006). Absent Structure. Introduction to Semiology (In Russian). – Moscow: Symposium, 2006.
50 Korneichuk B. (2015). The Role of Foreign Participation in Soviet Industrialization: Institutional Aspect. (In Russian) // Voprosy Economiki. 2015. №9.
51 Chernyavskay Y. (2010). Belarusians: from "tuteishya" to the nation. (In Russian) – Moscow: FUAinform, 2010. – 512 p.
52 Akudovich V. (2007). Code of Absence (the Basics of Belarusian Mentality) (In Belarusian). – Minsk: Logvinov, 2007. – 216 p.
53 Kudrinskiy F. (1904). Belarusians (General Overview) (In Russian) // Vilenskiy Calendar on 1905. Vilna: Typography: "Russian Pochin", 1904. – Pp. 108 – 116.
54 Shumskaya I. (2017). Cultural Matrix as a Way to Reveal National Mentality. (In Russian) // Istoricheskaya Pravda. 2017. – http://www.istpravda.ru/bel/research/6551/
55 Ibid.

56 Weis B.L. (2004). Same Soul, Many Bodies. Discover the Healing Power of Future Lives Through Progression Therapy. – Free Press, New York, 2004. – 227 p.
57 Kuperman A., Saygal N., Shiller A. (2017). Religion and National Identity in Central and Eastern Europe. (In Russian). // Pew Research Center, 2017. – 52 p.
58 Shumskaya I. (2017). Cultural Matrix as a Way to Reveal National Mentality. (In Russian) // Istoricheskaya Pravda. 2017. – http://www.istpravda.ru/bel/research/6551/
59 Kuperman A., Saygal N., Shiller A. (2017). Religion and National Identity in Central and Eastern Europe. (In Russian). // Pew Research Center, 2017. – 52 p.
60 Lashuk I. and others. (2016). Reproduction of Historical Memory in the Great Patriotic War in Public Opinion of Belarusians and Russians (In Russian). //. Institute of Socilogy of National Academy of Science, 2016.
61 Akudovich V. (2007). Code of Absence (the Basics of Belarusian Mentality) (In Belarusian). – Minsk: Logvinov, 2007. – 216 p.
62 Yurchak A. (2005) Everything Was Forever, Until It Was No More: The Last Soviet Generation. – Princeton University Press, 2005. – 352 p.
63 Mid M. (1988). Culture and the World of Childhood (In Russian). – Moscow: The Main Editorial of Eastern Literature "Science", 1988.
64 Yasin E. (2017). Development of Post-Soviet Economy: From Past to the Future. (In Russian) // Voprosy Economiki. 2017. №6. Pp. 5 – 21.
65 Levitsky S. (2010). Competitive Authoritarianism: Hybrid Regimes after the Cold War (Problems of International Politics). – Cambridge University Press, 2010. – 536 p.
66 Treisman D. (2012). The Return: Russia's Journey from Gorbachev to Medvedev. -/ Free Press, 2012. – 544 p.
67 Gorodnichenko Y., Roland G. (2011). Which Dimensions of Culture Matter for Long Run Growth. // American Economic Review Papers and Proceedings. 101 (2011). Pp. 492 – 498.
68 Gorodnichenko Y., Roland G. (2010). Culture, Institutions and The Wealth of Nations. - Working Paper No. 16368. National Bureau of Economic Research. Cambridge, MA. September 2010. – 51 p.
69 Gorodnichenko Y., Roland G. (2015). Culture, Institutions and Democratization. - Working Paper No. 21117. National Bureau of Economic Research. Cambridge, MA. April 2015. – 43 p.
70 Taleb N. N. (2007). The Black Swan: The Impact of Highly Improbable. / Random House. New York, 2007. – 366 p.
71 Beloveshkin A. (2016). Clear Biology – Why Businessmen Feel "Learned Helplessness" (In Russian) / https://people.onliner.by/opinions/2016/05/03/mnenie-438
72 Alexievich S. (2016). Secondhand Time: The Last of the Soviets. / Random House. - New York, 2016. – 496 p.

73 Mlodinow L. (2012). How Your Unconscious Mind Rules Your Behavior. – Vintage Books. A Division of Random House, Inc. New York, 2012. – 260 p.
74 Banerjee A., Duflo E. (2012). Poor Economics: A Radical Retinking of the Way to Fight Global Poverty. / Public Affairs, 2012. – 320 p.
75 Lu N. (2017). Ten Important Problems in the Field of Economic Management in the Period of Systemic Transformation in Russia (In Russian). // DVTEV. China. – 08.05 – 15.05.2017. – P. 5.
76 Mullainathan S., Sharif E. (2013). Scarcity. The New Science of Having Less and How it Defines Our Lives. Picador. New York, 2013. – 288 p.
77 Diamond J. (2019) Upheaval. Turning Points for Nations in Crisis. Little, Brown and Company. New York, 2019. – 502 p.
78 Easterly W. (2015). The Tyranny of Experts: Economists, Dictators and Forgotten Rights of the Poor. / Basic Books, 2015. – 416 p.
79 Snyder T. (2018). The Road to Unfreedom. Russia, Europe, America. – Vintage. London, 2018. – 359 p.
80 Reich R. (2013). Aftershock: the Next Economy and America's Future. – Vintage, 2013. – 288 p.
81 Diamond J. (2005). Guns, Germs and Steel. The Fate of Human Societies. / W.W. Norton & Company, 2005. – 528 p.
82 Kapelushnikov R. (2013). Behavioral Economy and New Paternalism. (In Russian) Moscow, Publishing House: High School of Economics, 2013.
83 Lashuk I. and others. (2016). Reproduction of Historical Memory in the Great Patriotic War in Public Opinion of Belarusians and Russians (In Russian). //. Institute of Socilogy of National Academy of Science, 2016.
84 Ibid.
85 Edachev A., Natkhov A., Polischuk L. (2016). War and Values: Experience of Empirical Analysis (In Russian). // Voprosy Economiki. 2016. №3. Pp. 5 – 33.
86 Mikoyan A.I.. (1999). That's How It Was. (In Russian) – Moscow.: Vagrius, 1999. – 638 p.
87 UNDP (2015). National Human Development Report. – UNDP, The Republic of Belarus, 2015.
88 Kuperman A., Saygal N., Shiller A. (2017). Religion and National Identity in Central and Eastern Europe. (In Russian). // Pew Research Center, 2017. – 52 p.
89 Lashuk I. (2015). Transformation of the Family in the Modern Belarusian Society (Base on the Sociological Survey). (In Russian) // Institute of Sociology of the National Academy of Science, 2015.
90 Rudy K. (2015). Gender Factors of Economic Growth in Belarus. (In Russian) // Belorusskiy Economicheskiy Journal. – 2015. - №4. – Pp.23-32.
91 Sharma R. (2016). The Rise and Fall of Nations: Forces of Change in the Post Crisis World. / W.W. Norton & Company, 2016. – 466 p.
92 Deutscher G. (2016). Through the Mirror of the Language. Why the World Look Different in Other Languages. (In Russian) – Moscow: ACT, 2016.

93 Gladwell M. (2011) Outliers: The Story of Success. – Little, Brown and Company. – New York, 2011. – 336 p.
94 Lashuk I. (2016). Social Stereotypes of CIS in the Masses of Belarusians (In Russian) //Institute Sociology of the National Academy of Science of Belarus, 2016.
95 Botsman R. (2016). We've stopped trusting institutions and started trusting strangers. / TED. – October 2016.
96 Rickards J. (2014). The Death of Money: The Coming Collapse of International Monetary System. / Portfolio, 2014. – 368 p.
97 Lewis M. (2011). Boomerang: Travels in a New Third World. / W.W.Norton and Company. - New York, 2011. – 224 p.
98 Shmygov V., Vlasov D. (2016). How were Devaluated Belarusian Ruble and other Currencies of ex-Soviet Countries (In Russian). – http://finance.tut.by/news481757.html
99 Ross A. (2016). The Industries of the Future. How the Next 10 Years of Innovation will Transform Our Lives at Work and Home. – Simon & Schuster. London. 2016. – 304 p.
100 Sharma R. (2016). The Rise and Fall of Nations: Forces of Change in the Post Crisis World. / W.W. Norton & Company, 2016. – 466 p.
101 Ford M. (2015). The Rise of the Robots. Technology and the Threat of Mass Unemployment. – One World, 2015. – 334 p.
102 Speer A. (1998). Memoirs. (In Russian) – Moscow: Rusich, 1998. – 700 p.
103 Guiso L., Sapienzia P., Zingales L. (2006). Does Culture Affect Economic Outcomes? - National Bureau of Economic Research. January 2002. Working paper 11999.
104 Rudy K., Bobrovich V., Lashuk I., Urban D. (2018) "Middle-Income Trap": Interdisciplinary Evaluation of the Way Out for Belarus. (In Russian) // Belorusskiy Economicheskiy Journal. – 2018. - №3. – Pp. 4 – 18.
105 Life in Transition Survey. (2016) — EBRD, 2016.
106 Based on IPM opinion polls in 2006, 2008, 2018. – www.ipm.by
107 Ibid.
108 Ibid.
109 Ibid.
110 Ibid.
111 Pinker S. (2018). Enlightenment Now. The Case for Reason, Science, Humanism and Progress / S. Pinker. – NY: Penguin, 2018. – 524 p.
112 Welzel Ch. (2013). Freedom Rising: Human Empowerment and the Quest for Emancipation. / Cambridge University Press, 2013. – 472 p.
113 Sapsford, R., Abbott, P., Haerpfer, C., & Wallace, C. (2015). Trust in Post-Soviet Countries, Ten Years On. European Politics and Society, 16(4), 523-539.
114 Safina D. (2015). Trust and Economic Growth in Russian society. // Procedia Economics and finance. 24, 2015. Pp. 563 – 567.
115 Based on IPM opinion polls in 2006, 2008, 2018. – www.ipm.by

116 Based on the data from Institute of Sociology from National Academy of Science of Belarus.
117 Kotlyarov I. And others. (2017). Belarusian Society in the Context of Cultural Code: Sociological Survey (In Russian). – Minsk, Belarusian Thought. – 2017.
118 Based on the data from Institute of Sociology from National Academy of Science of Belarus.
119 Mullainathan S., Sharif E. (2013). Scarcity. The New Science of Having Less and How it Defines Our Lives. Picador. New York, 2013. – 288 p.
120 Banerjee A., Duflo E. (2012). Poor Economics: A Radical Rethinking of the Way to Fight Global Poverty. / Public Affairs, 2012. – 320 p.
121 Balasubramanyam V.N., Salisu M., Sapsford D. (1996). Foreign direct investment and growth in EP and IS countries. // The Economic Journal. Vol. 106. No. 434. Pp. 92 – 105.
122 Borensztein E., Gregorio J., Lee J.-W. (1998). How does foreign direct investment affect economic growth? // Journal of International Economics. Vol. 45. No. 1. Pp. 115 – 135.
123 Xu B. (2000). Multinational enterprises, technology division, and host country productivity growth. // Journal of Development Economics. Vol. 62. No. 2, pp. 477 – 493.
124 Banerjee A.V., Duflo E. (2019). Good Economics for Hard Times. – Public Affairs, NY. – 2019. – 403 p.
125 Jude C., Leviege G. (2013). Growth effect of FDI in developing economies: the role of institutional quality. // MPRA Paper No. 49321.
126 Gorodnichenko Y., Svejnar J., Terell K. (2014). When Does FDI Have Positive Spillovers? Evidence from 17 Transition Market Economies. // Journal of Comparative Economics. 42 (2014). Pp. 954 – 969.
127 Kunnapas, K. (2013). R&D Tax Incentives in a Small Economy – An Estonian Example. Tallin University of Technology.
128 Doing Business Annual Report. / https://www.doingbusiness.org/content/dam/doingBusiness/country/b/belarus/BLR.pdf
129 Belarus in Numbers: Statistics (In Russian) (2017). / National Statistical Committee of the Republic of Belarus. – Minsk: National Statistical Committee of the Republic of Belarus, 2017. – 72 p.
130 Ibid.
131 Ibid.
132 Sharma R. (2016). The Rise and Fall of Nations: Forces of Change in the Post Crisis World. / W.W. Norton & Company, 2016. – 466 p.
133 Ross A. (2016). The Industries of the Future. How the Next 10 Years of Innovation will Transform Our Lives at Work and Home. – Simon & Schuster. London. 2016. – 304 p.

134 Bremmer I. (2010). The End of Free Market. Who Wins the War Between States and Corporations? – Portfolio, 2010. – 240 p.
135 Mlodinow L. (2012). How Your Unconscious Mind Rules Your Behavior. – Vintage Books. A Division of Random House, Inc. New York, 2012. – 260 p.
136 Based on data by the Ministry of Foreign Affairs of Belarus.
137 Reich R. (2013). Aftershock: the Next Economy and America's Future. – Vintage, 2013. – 288 p.
138 Based on the data from Institute of Sociology from National Academy of Science of Belarus.
139 Ibid.
140 Ibid.
141 Ibid.
142 Ibid.
143 Regions of Belarus (Part 1): Statistics (In Russian) (2016) / National Statistical Committee of the Republic of Belarus. – Minsk: National Statistical Committee of the Republic of Belarus, 2016. – 774 p.
144 Based on the data from Institute of Sociology from National Academy of Science of Belarus.
145 Ibid.
146 Opros "Delovoy klimat v Respublike Belarus 2013", (2013). RDWB, 2013, Repräentanz der Deutschen Wirtschaft in Belarus.
147 Kovalev M., Wang S. (2015). China is Making Knowledge Economy (In Russian) /Minsk: BSU, 2015. – 152 p.
148 Acemoglu D. (2015). The World Our Grandchildren Will Inherit. / In 100 Years. Leading Economists Predict the Future. – The MIT Press. London, 2015. – Pp. 1 – 35.
149 Ford M. (2015). The Rise of the Robots. Technology and the Threat of Mass Unemployment. – One World, 2015. – 334 p.
150 Ross A. (2016). The Industries of the Future. How the Next 10 Years of Innovation will Transform Our Lives at Work and Home. – Simon & Schuster. London. 2016. – 304 p.
151 Cruickshank D. (2017). Global Manufacturing "Back to the Future". // Caijing. Annual Edition. – 2017. – Pp.72 – 74.
152 Ford M. (2015). The Rise of the Robots. Technology and the Threat of Mass Unemployment. – One World, 2015. – 334 p.
153 Brautigam D., Tang X. (2013) "Going Global in Groups": Structural Transformation and Chinese Economic Zones Overseas. // World Development. 2013. P. 1 – 14.
154 Rudy K (2016) Belarus – China: Channels for Investment Cooperation. (In Russian) // Beloruskiy Economicheskiy Journal. – 2016. - №4. – Pp.23-32.
155 Rudy K. (2012). Possibilities to Attract Capital from Chinese Financial Market to Belarus (In Russian) // Bankovskiy Vestnik 2012. №22. Pp. 25 – 31.

156 Saakashvili M., Bendukidze K. (2014). Georgia. The Most Radical Catch-Up Reforms. / The Great Rebirth. Lessons from the Victory of Capitalism over Communism. – Peterson Institute for International Economics. Washington, 2014. P. 149 – 163.
157 Drozdov V., Rudy K. (2005). Social and Economic Transformation of Market Economies (In Russian) // Mir Peremen. 2005. №4. Pp. 114-125.
158 Index of Economic Freedom (2017). - http://www.heritage.org/index/
159 Ibid.
160 Based on Wikipedia – www.wikipedia.org
161 Eichengreen B., Rose A.K., Wyplosz Ch. (1996). Contangious Currency Crises. - Working Paper No. 5681. National Bureau of Economic Research. Cambridge, MA. July 1996. – 48 p
162 Masson P. (1998). Contagion: Monsoonal Effects, Spillovers, and Jumps between Multiple Equilibria. – IMF Working Paper 98/142. 1998. – 54 p.
163 Samarasinha S. (2017). Changing hearts and minds to save people and planet. – TEDxNiamiha. March 25, 2017.
https://www.youtube.com/watch?v=7_hFmRzffOg
164 Kuperman A., Saygal N., Shiller A. (2017). Religion and National Identity in Central and Eastern Europe. (In Russian). // Pew Research Center, 2017. – 52 p.
165 Florida R., Mellander C., King K. (2015). The Global Creativity Index 2015, 68p. – http://www.martinprosperity.org
166 Saxena N.C. (2011). Virtuous Cycles: The Singapore Public Service and National Development. / Civil Service College, MFA Singapore, UNDP. 2011, 200 p.
167 Florida R., Mellander C., King K. (2015). The Global Creativity Index 2015, 68p. – http://www.martinprosperity.org
168 Index of Economic Freedom (2017). - http://www.heritage.org/index/
169 Global Competitiveness Report. (2017) –
http://www3.weforum.org/docs/WEF_TheGlobalCompetitivenessReport2017.pdf
170 Palacios-Huerta I. (2013). In 100 Years: Leading Economists Predict the Future. / ed. by Palacios-Huerta I. – The MIT Press, 2013. – 195 p.
171 Friedman G. (2010). The Next Decade. Empire and Republic in a Changing World. – Anchor Books. New York, 2010. – 243 p.
172 Friedman G. (2010). The Next 100 Years. A Forecast for the 21st Century. – Anchor Books. New York, 2010. – 253 p.
173 Lewis M. (2015). Flash Boys: A Wall Street Revolt. – W.W.Norton Company, 2015. – 320 p.
174 Kelly K. (2016). The Inevitable. Understanding the 12 technological forces that will shape our future. – Viking, NY, 2016. – 356 p.
175 Zhang Chunlin (2017). How to Prevent Social Polarization Caused by Technological Progress. // Caijing. Annual Edition. – 2017. – Pp.54 – 61.

176 Ford M. (2015). The Rise of the Robots. Technology and the Threat of Mass Unemployment. – One World, 2015. – 334 p.
177 Barrat J. (2013). Our Final Invention: Artificial Intelligence and the End of the Human Era. – Thomas Dunne. New York, 2013.
178 The Economist. (2016). The Return of the Machinery Question. / The Economist, June 25th, 2016. Pp. 3 – 16.
179 Barberis N., Thaler R. (2002). A Survey of Behavioral Finance. / NBER, Working Paper 9222, September 2002. – 78 p.
180 The Economist. (2016). The Return of the Machinery Question. / The Economist, June 25th, 2016. Pp. 3 – 16.
181 The Economist. (2015). Hot and Bothered. Special Report. Climate Change. / The Economist, November 28th, 2015. Pp. 3 – 16.
182 Friedman T.L. (2016). Thank You for Being Late: An Optimist's Guide to Thriving in the Age of Accelerations. / Farrar, 2016. – 496 p.
183 The Economist. (2017). Learning and earning. Special Report. Lifelong Education. / The Economist, January 14th, 2017. Pp. 1 – 14.
184 Shanmugaratnam T. (2017). BBC HARDTalk: Singapore's DPM, grilled by Steven Sackur. – https://www.youtube.com/watch?v=YOtlNZN2ZVg
185 Bee Wah Tan, Chor Foon Tang. (2016). Examining the Causal Linkages among Domestic Investment, FDI, Trade, Interest Rate and Economic Growth in ASEAN-5 Countries. International Journal of Economics and Financial Issues, 6(1): 214-220.
186 Rapaille C. (2015). The Culture Code: An Ingenious Way to Understand Why People Around the World Live and Buy as They Do. / Crown Business, 2015. – 224 p.
187 Rapaille C. (2015). The Global Code: How a New Culture of Universal Values is Reshaping Business and Marketing. / St. Martin's Press, 2015. – 304 p.
188 The Economist. (2015). Hot and Bothered. Special Report. Climate Change. / The Economist, November 28th, 2015. Pp. 3 – 16.
189 Samarasinha S. (2017). Changing hearts and minds to save people and planet. – TEDxNiamiha. March 25, 2017.
https://www.youtube.com/watch?v=7_hFmRzffOg
190 Alexievich S. (2017). Boys in Zink. – Penguin Popular Classic, 2017.
191 Rudy K. and others (2016). Financial Diet: Reforms of Public Finance in Belarus (In Russian) – Minsk: Zvyazda, 2016. – 464 p.
192 Rudy K. And others (2017). «Because We Decided So": Behavioral Economy of Belarus and Its Decoding. (In Russian) – Minsk: Zvyazda, 2017. – 368 p.
193 Kahneman D. (2013) Thinking, Fast and Slow. / Farrar, Straus and Giroux. New York, 2013. – 499 p.
194 Thaler R. (2016). Misbehaving: The Making of Behavioral Economics. – W.W. Norton & Company, 2016. – 432 p.
195 Thaler R., Sunstein C. (2009). Nudge: Improving Decisions about Health, Wealth and Happiness. Penguin Books, 2009.

196 Tversky A. (2003). Preference, Belief, and Similarity: Selected Writings (MIT Press). – A Bradford Book, 2003. – 1039 p.